Finding Chris,

My Father

Vincent Ellis White

Life.Love.Religion Publishing
www.lifelovereligion.com

Presents

Finding Chris, My Father

A Coming of Age Memoir of Confusion, Abandonment, & Fatherlessness, which lead to Faith in Abundance, Family Togetherness, & Ultimate Triumph

Written By: Vincent Ellis White

From the Internet radio host of the highly popular "Vincent Ellis White Show" on www.Ishoutforjoy.com reemerges the truth-telling author of the explosive, best-selling breakout novel: *The Fully-Seasoned Man's Relationship Recipe [Men's Confessional/Women's Tutorial]* (2010), and the inspirational, heartfelt book: *L.L.R. Inspirations: From the Cellar of my Soul* (2010).

Published by:

Vincent Ellis White/Life Love Religion Publishing

http://www.lifelovereligion.com

Email: llrpublishing@yahoo.com

http://www.facebook.com/TheVincentEllisWhiteShow

Twitter: @LifeLoveRVA

Printed in the USA by

Lightning Source

ISBN-10: 0615578853

ISBN-13: 978-0-615-57885-9

Finding Chris, My Father

Vincent Ellis White

This memoir is a 100% true story. Nothing is fiction or has been fabricated for the sake of sales, suspense, or future fame. This is my life and proof that God is still in the miracle working business. I thank my Lord, Jesus Christ, every day for such a miracle, especially when I receive a call from my father, or make a call to him, and especially when we can see each other in person. I love you, Dad-Mr. Chris Anderson. Remember, "Smooth like me."

~Vincent Ellis White

Table of Contents

Dedication:

This memoir is dedicated to my past family, my blood family, my church family, and my future family to be. To God be the glory.

-Vincent Ellis White

About the Author

Vincent Ellis White, 31, is a Richmond, Va. native who has accomplished plenty in his short lifespan. He obtained his Master's in Education from Strayer University (2010); Bachelors in Mass Communication from Norfolk State University (2002); and his high school diploma from Meadowbrook High School in Richmond, Va. (1998).

He is the highly controversial, truth-telling Internet radio host of the popular "Vincent Ellis White Show" on www.Ishoutforjoy.com. He has written/published two books thus far: Publish-America's best-selling ***The Fully-Seasoned Man's Relationship Recipe*** (2010), ***L.L.R. Inspirations: From the Cellar of my Soul*** (2010), and is currently in the process of preparing his mighty and evolutionary poetic endeavor entitled, ***Poetic Evolution***. He became a *Style Weekly* magazine, Top 40 under 40 (in his native city of Richmond, Va.) award-winning recipient in the year 2010, an IShoutforJoy Top 35 under 35 Recipient in 2011, and has appeared on numerous radio shows/events throughout the U.S. Along with being an accomplished author, poet, self-publisher, mentor, and counselor, his most prized love is being an outstanding role model and father to his son, Jordan Ellis White. He dedicates all of his success to his Lord and Savior, Jesus Christ, and has no shame in the fact that he is a Christian, yet comes from a very tainted past. He is one who speaks with such candor, reveals a transparent soul, and is willing to share his testimony with the world, hoping that it will uplift all those who come into his path.

FOREWORDS Written by Mr. Duron Chavis

"Brother Manifest"

I want the reader to take a moment. Relax. Close your eyes. Imagine your child bundled close to your back. The child's soft breathing against your back. It's very survival dependent upon you. Now imagine a ravenous beast. Fangs bared. Claws extended. Bloodlust in its eyes. Stalking you and your child as its prey. Imagine yourself with your child in arm as this beast approaches you. Look behind you. Imagine the only thing behind you is a bottomless chasm. There is nowhere to run.

The protection for you stands in front, between you and that beast. He is your husband, the father of the child you hold. His mission is to protect you from this beast and prevent you from falling into that bottomless chasm. He has battled many prior adversaries in defense of his family. He is fearless. Determined. Committed to the survival of his wife and child. Nothing will stand in his way. Now imagine him weapon at ready as that beast lunges forth! Imagine the sinews of his arms, the sun's glimmer off his back, and the look of terror in the beast's face! He is your warrior.

The beast is the society we live in. A by-product of racism, discrimination and mis-education, and the chasm behind you is poverty and crime. The problem is that for all too many black families that warrior is absent, leaving the family unit at an extreme disadvantage. Imagine the beast lunging at you again without that warrior to protect you and your child.

Fatherlessness is the key issue we must focus on in developing solutions for decreasing disparities in the black community. Families exist as social structures that increase the stability of the community we are a part of. When any one aspect of the family comes up missing, it is our responsibility to compensate for that absence, especially as it relates to the natural parents. As a result of high incarceration rates, high divorce rates, high murder rates, high health disparity rates, and high poverty rates, we often find the black man missing from the family unit. – The mother attempts to play a duel role of mom and dad, while working extended hours in order to provide for the family or reliant upon government programs residing in highly toxic environments surrounded by crime, drugs, and various other pathologies.

Relationships are never walks in the park. They require love and nurturance in order to flourish. The initial stages are sublime, both parties actively engaged in the newness of one another's company-the freshness of ideas shared, the vigor and passion of the interaction fueled by curiosity and maintained by the desire to explore the other person and enjoy their company. Time is the best judge of character because without the right tools, a relationship can get rocky. Some relationships stand the test of time; however, many end, especially in the African-American community where women have the highest rate of divorce and the lowest rate of marriage.

Navigating the end of a relationship is a difficult task, wrought with numerous obstacles. The most treacherous of these not listed in order of importance include ego, distrust, financial issues, and the pain of heartbreak, just to name a few. Two individuals going their separate ways can be difficult enough, but imagine the complexity of ending one where children are involved. There are a multitude of consequences that neither party will consider that explicitly affect a specific segment of the U.S. population. Arguably, the consequences of family fragmentation, in general, and a father's absence, in specific, create a cycle of pathology that systematically reproduces the problem and its consequences.

Certainly it must become our practice as a community to speak clearly and honestly about our role in perpetuating cycles of pathology, such as fatherlessness. Men, as well as women, play integral roles in the sustenance of co-parenting post dissolution of marriages and long-term relationships. Take into consideration that a great many children in the African-American community are born out of wedlock. You do not have to think long to understand why other ethnicities that do not have similar rates of family fragmentation control the majority of the businesses that operate in our community. Other ethnicities appear to have strong considerations toward legacy building, independence, and family that curb much of the pathological behavior that causes family fragmentation. Ironically, a surge in single-parent households and incarceration occurred simultaneously with the Civil Rights Movement and has steadily skyrocketed since the 1960's. Perhaps there were values embedded in the social fabric of the African-American community that were lost once desegregation laws were passed and urban renewal projects ran highways through black communities all across the United States.

According to the Richmond Family and Fatherhood Initiative, broken families in Richmond, VA cost U.S. taxpayers over 200 million dollars. If scrutinized as an economic issue alone, one can surmise that a father's absence in the black community plays a huge role in the cycle of poverty experienced by many in the African-American community. The money spent by the U.S. taxpayer on Social Service programs such as Medicaid and food stamps, not to mention Temporary Assistance for Needy Families (TANF), the criminal justice system, housing programs, etc., would reduce immensely via the financial stability inherent in two-parent households with parents working together to ensure the future necessary for the success of their children; however, to view fatherlessness through a financial lens alone is not a holistic approach to reality. An accurate assessment would include the sociological, cultural, and health impact, an impact that manifests itself in virtually every major urban center throughout the United States.

Eighty percent of all African-American children can now expect to spend a significant part of their childhood living apart from their fathers. Adding insult to injury, the National Urban League reports boys who grow up without fathers are more likely to become unmarried fathers themselves at a young age. Girls growing up without fathers are more likely to have sex at an early age and become pregnant while a teenager. Boys raised in single parent homes are more likely to commit a crime leading to incarceration. This epidemic of fatherlessness has surged since the 1960's. Since 1960, the proportion of black children living with a single parent more than doubled, from 22% to 53.3% in 2000. A study done in 1992 in Texas showed that 85% of the youth incarcerated were from fatherless homes showing a direct correlation between having one's father and not becoming a product of the prison industrial complex.

The responsibility for preventing fatherlessness falls into the hands of both parents; however, it is primarily the role of the father to surmount any and all obstacles placed in his path to become a part of his child's life, notwithstanding the impasse of the mother herself. Mothers must realize that they cannot withhold parental involvement by virtue of their egotistic wants and selfish needs. There are one too many stories of women who use their children as bartering chips to force men to submit to their emotional whims and/or financial desires. Such abuse of authority is paramount to child neglect, leaving many a father without option or without recourse except the emotionally stagnating and financially draining family court custody case which often sides with the mother. This becomes a by-product of a society that values the role of the mother as a parent more so than that of the father when both ideally are of equal importance to the identity and social stability of the child in question. Your child must know his/her father. This is not optional. The consequences are too great for him/her not to know. God forbid you, as a parent, would become a wall between your child and his paternal lineage. Fathers have to develop the maturity and determination that will not allow them to walk out on their children's lives regardless of what the circumstances may be. All too often, men find themselves in financial and legal struggles resultant from poor education and lack of job training; however, those obstacles are not insurmountable nor reason to divorce yourself from your children as well.

Fathers must make their children the number one priority in their lives in order to break the cycle. You can't make time to watch the game or go to the club or for recreational drug use or to play video games while your child is at home with his/her mother facing the world with only one piece of its puzzle in place. Nor can you presume that your child support payment alone is sufficient to warrant your absence emotionally and socially. Your child needs your guidance, your consistent presence, and your insight on what it means to be a man. He/she needs a positive male example, and you as the natural father are the first example they will know. Do not relinquish your responsibility.

The irony of such an issue plaguing the African-American community is that the most effective tool used by our people to combat the traumatizing effects of slavery, discrimination, and Jim Crow was a stable family unit.

In order to discourage rebellion and disconnect our ancestors from their original cultures and further indoctrinate them generation after generation into the social institution of enslavement, enslaved Africans were sold away from Africans from the same village and region. Plantation owners would further attempt to prevent disobedience amid enslaved Africans with the threat of selling away "wives" and children. Today, instead of having our families separated by force, we are willing participants in a practice that was once used to oppress our people.

Think about it. Our ancestors used to brave life and limb in order to maintain traditional structures that we take for granted today. Punishment for running away would be a lashing from the overseer's whip or dismemberment, i.e., cutting off a foot or hand. Despite such cruelty, hundreds of thousands of enslaved Africans ran away from plantations yearly, many to be reunited with family members who had been sold to other plantations throughout the country. Are we honoring the sacrifices of those who came before us in our quickness to end relationships where there are children involved? How disrespectful is it to our ancestors to not be involved as the father of your child or to prevent the father of your child from being involved in that child's upbringing? If we do not owe it to those who came before us, do we not owe it to those who came after us?

The fact that so many single-parent households exist, specifically in the black community, is hard to swallow. There is room for an even deeper analysis of this issue in the many tomes of research that has been done by social scientists, but nothing trumps the fact that black women must be applauded for making miracles happen on a daily basis. The absence of black fathers in the home has not stopped the innumerable successes, though we all know that our community can do better. The fact is we will do better, and by addressing issues such as this now and making wise decisions regarding co-parenting, mate selection, and family planning, we will continue to build the future that those who come after us deserve.

In *"Finding Chris, My Father,"* you will develop an understanding of one man's quest to reconnect with his father. This unique and dynamic testimony of struggle and growing up black and male without his biological father is amazing, giving firsthand testimony of the effects of fatherlessness on African-American males. Our responsibility is to do all that we can to break the cycle. We owe it to those who will come after us and to those who sacrificed so that we may be here today.

-Duron Chavis "Brother Manifest"

"My special Christmas present doesn't hold a place under the tree. It is not wrapped in beautiful paper or tied with a fancy bow. I don't have to worry if it's the right color or if it fits, but it comes in two parts."

-Mom

Dec. 25th, 2007

Christmas has always been such an unforgettable and memorable time of year for me. I've always been one who was able to recall specifics about each, because dates/times are so significant to me. I remember this one so vividly; it was around 8:40 a.m. It was me, my younger brother, my grandmother, and my mom. We had all just begun to sort through the pile of presents that lay dormant under the Christmas tree.

As usual, around my house on this day excitement filled the air. Christmas breakfast was already cooking, and you could smell the aroma from all the way upstairs. As a matter of fact, I believe it is what originally woke me up, along with the excitement of the holiday. You see, even being 27 years old, I still get hyped up about Christmas as if I was still that snotty-nosed kid at age 10 who couldn't even get to sleep due to thinking about what Santa Claus was going to bring me the next morning. Needless to say, I still woke up extra early. I would still go wake up all my family members and tell them: "C'mon, iiiittttttt'ssssss Chhhrrriisssssttmmaaassss" (singing). I was and still am that guy.

After sorting, sifting, maneuvering, and mentally labeling all of my gifts into my special corner, I began to watch as others were already opening their gifts. For some strange reason, I like to wait until others have at least opened a few gifts first before I truly begin.

I watched as my brother, 14 years old at the time, was getting everything he had asked for, everything he wanted. He received the five pairs of sneakers that he previously desired, the three video games that he'd had his eye on, the Carolina Panthers sports jacket, gloves, hat, and even slippers that I knew would make him go bonkers, and many apparel outfits to get him right for his return to high school after winter break. He was cheesing hard, and rightfully he should be. He pretty much had received everything he'd asked for at some point in the year.

My mother received some pretty good gifts, too. She'd gotten an armoire, some jewelry, a poem, and an African statue from me, two very comfortable robes, money, and a bill paid. I can't say for sure whether she got everything she'd asked for or desired, but she was very content and happy.

I began to open some of my gifts, while also watching the others. I opened one, and it was a Kenneth Cole watch that I had my eye on from Hecht's. I thanked my mother, as I watched out of the corner of my eye my granny opening her few gifts. She was never that excited when opening them, but I assumed she always got what she wanted because she didn't desire much but to be with those who she loved-her family. I opened one, then two, then gift after gift. I began to dance around causing everyone to laugh hysterically at my antics. I was a kidder for sure, and everyone knew it. I always got some amazing gifts every Christmas, though my mother would always be struggling throughout the year (especially Christmastime). Somehow, she always found a way to make this holiday extra special to her children. I was definitely appreciative. I had received everything from a Kenneth Cole watch, to Norfolk State jacket (my Alma Mater, in which I love), some Jordan sneakers, money, Sean John (my favorite label) top hat and more.

There was still one gift lying there that my mother told me to open upstairs alone somewhere. I wondered what it was, but wasn't too pressed about it. She was always known to do surprises surrounding her more "bigger" gifts, so I honestly thought nothing of it. Grandma was finished with her gifts, my brother was finished with his gifts and had already snuck off upstairs to get started on the video games (which was typical), and my mother was about to finalize breakfast, so I figured this was the perfect time to zip upstairs and see what this hush-hush gift was going to be. It didn't look appealing at all; it was just an envelope with something heavy in it, something entirely too heavy to be inside an envelope. Regardless, I took it upstairs and slipped into the first part of our bathroom for some privacy. I wasn't nervous, because as I stated, she does this type of thing every other year. I thought I'd open this envelope and it would be a small gift, lined with a note or two, telling me to search in some weird spots of the house to find the remainder of my gift. Man, was I wrong!

I sat down in the bathroom and prepared myself to open this "gift." I cracked the envelope seal, and there was no gift, but rather a small, pint-sized journal. Shocked and confused, I opened the journal and began to read. There were some pages folded over, and I could see my mother's big handwriting all throughout the back of the pages coming through the front. The first page read, "My special Christmas present doesn't hold a place under the tree. It is not wrapped in beautiful paper or tied with a fancy bow. I don't have to worry if it's the right color or if it fits, but it comes in two parts." I wondered what the two parts would entail.

As I started to read, the first part began with my mother apologizing for "shortchanging" some things throughout my life. I immediately started to allow my eyes to follow my thoughts, as they began rolling round and round. I was thinking to myself, I've heard this all before countless times. I was also thinking, why is this even a "gift?" Still slightly intrigued, I kept reading. She went into further detail about how she apologizes for making a decision that has affected my life for over 16 years, for the times that I've felt anger towards her because of her decision, and that she always had this one regret and piece of guilt that kept burning her up, which was that she never told me about my biological father.

Well, let me take that back a step. She did tell me about him, but it wasn't until I was 16 years old that she did. As you can imagine, that sent me topsy-turvy! Anyway, I didn't feel like hearing this again (nor reading it), because it just makes me mad every time. There was more, and as I dove deeper inside those pages I found out such.

After being so apologetic, she went on talking about how she was glad that I at least had Pa-Pa (her father) in my life to make a difference, and she also expressed that she had been forgiven by God, yet she never felt she was forgiven by me fully (in which she wasn't). She further explained that she knows she was wrong, and at the time she thought it was the right thing to do, etc., etc., etc. ("etc." is what it sounded like to me). She continued with the all too familiar story that I've heard more than a few times, about how she'd researched him, Googled him, had the Richmond Department of Social Services search for him, and had private eyes seek him out, all only to find nothing. Zero. Zilch. She even said that sometimes they would call her back saying that they've found him. She would come running downtown to Social Services, only to be greeted by a white man (obviously, who was not my biological father)! At this moment, I was speed reading, because I knew this story and didn't like the ending. I never got what I wanted from the ending. The next page (which was folded in a triangle) said, "Hopefully, this will fix things between you and me …." At that very moment, I was nervous to turn the page…but something inside me forced my fingers to do the turning.

The next page turned over. I saw something that was enough to send thousands of electric volts through my body (it felt like that, at least). It was Part Two. It began with a short story dating back to the previous Wednesday when my mother went to visit my grandmother in the hospital (who was sick with emphysema and pneumonia). She wrote that she was planning on going to my grandmother's house first to check on it since she had been in the hospital for so long, but she couldn't get over to take the Forest Hill exit to her house; therefore, she ended up having to keep straight (to the hospital). She wrote that it had to be God, because of how He intervened. She stated that if she was able to get over on that particular street, then she would have missed the big surprise that she was about to get. The words seemed like they began to shake, but I was just getting anxious. I wanted to know what the hell she had found that she had to write in this journal, seal it in this envelope, and call it a "gift." I kept reading.

The words increased in size and began to become more intriguing. It read that she was walking down the hallway in Chippenham Hospital leading her towards my grandmother's room, when she saw a man walking towards her who looked familiar. She said he was short, about 5'7, 5'8, brown-skinned, attractive, grayish hair, had on the uniform that a doctor would wear, and was strutting a little bit. I immediately began to get jealous, because I don't like my mother looking at any man. (Overprotective, I thought she was saying she had an attraction to this man, but she was simply setting the scene!) She said that their eyes met, they smiled cunningly, and that her heart immediately began to flutter at an alarming rate. She called it "instant gratification." This was the end of the page, so I had to turn yet another folded up page. I did so.

She further wrote that as he passed, and she stared more, she noticed that ....this man walking passed her was CHRIS! CHRIS ANDERSON! She said that she immediately had to "hit him with his Christmas present." Understand, he didn't know he even had a child, so as you can imagine, this was about to turn into a shocker for not just my mother, but for him as well. She grabbed him by the shoulder

(to stop him from walking) and said aggressively, "Chris Anderson!!"
Startled, he took a good look at her and responded with her name,
"Belinda." As I read on, she continued to say to him "I had your
child 27 years ago." She said that he looked at her and said, "What!
Wait a minute. Let's go over here and sit down" smiling.

She then went into her explanation to him of why she made
the decision not to tell him (because they had already broken up) and
that she had always felt that she made the worst decision of her life
by not telling him and choosing to raise me on her own. She said that
she even apologized to him for the first time. After that shocking
revelation, she then began to give Chris some details about me.

As I read this, I had no feeling in my hands, and my mind
was on autopilot. She walked him to her car to show him a picture of
me, and he simply said, "Uh-huh" (but he was smiling she stated).
There was surely more for me to absorb in that little black book (like
how she told him she had "no problem with any test that's needed"),
but I had to stop reading after that. I got lightheaded. My jaw
dropped. The room got fuzzy. My hands got shaky. Was I really

reading what I think I was reading? Was this my "gift" she was hiding from me since last Wednesday?

I swear everything went black at that exact moment after I turned that page, only to see the name CHRIS ANDERSON in all caps and black bold. Figuratively, it screamed at me, loudly. If you're wondering did I know the name? Yes. I didn't know him, not at all, but I knew the name all too well.

When she told me at the tender age of 16 years old, the life-shattering, life-altering, devastating news of Mr. "Chris Anderson" being my biological father, I took it all in. Of course, I went through all the emotions from screaming, to kicking, to crying, to acting like I didn't give a crap, to many more; most importantly, I stored the name in my head-Chris Anderson. From the age of 16 to 27, I held that name in my head like it was the last thing I could keep before leaving this earth. For years, whenever I heard that name (which was everywhere), I would immediately turn around and look, only to be disappointed time and time again. I even had it in my head that I'd never meet him since no one has had any luck thus far, but I still kept it in my head.

Now, as I fast forward to this December 25, 2007 Christmas day, here comes my mother saying that she has found CHRIS ANDERSON (in bold). WHAT!?!?! Everything went black. I yelled out loudly, "WWWWHHHAAATTTT???" I just dropped the little book that held my entire life's desires inside. I dropped the book on the bathroom floor, and it sprawled open to the page that read "CHRIS ANDERSON!!" "How convenient," I thought to myself. Had I finally gotten what I wanted, what I needed, and what I desired?

This was the greatest gift a person could ever receive. I just couldn't fathom this ever happening. Severely shocked, confused, flabbergasted, relieved, and gravely thankful to God, I sat all alone in that bathroom. I just cried…and cried…and cried….

Summer 1986

"My name is Vincent Lopez Mapp III, and I am six years old." I would recite this as robotically as I possibly could when older folks would ask me my name and age. I would say it and smile. My smile always suggested that life was good for me, and for a childlike mind like mine, for the most part it was. In my mind, my daddy was away at school, and I had my mommy right there with me all day, every day. I was an only child at this time and loving every minute of it.

It was the summer time, and I distinctively remember how my mother and I would always go to the school where my Daddy studied so that we could spend some time with him. I was always excited to go to that school. I was always prepared to recite my line if anyone asked me (and they always did). I remember the ride was the longest ride ever. It felt like eternity, but I believe it was just over an hour.

My thoughts fade in and out as I try to rekindle them, but I do remember those park benches. I also remember that all of my dad's friends were the coolest. They would either have their pants legs rolled up, walk with a slow bop, have on a mean face that told me they meant business, or they would just say the coolest things. The park benches were rugged and brownish, and there was always a piece or two missing from the part where we'd sit.

My mother would let me run to my daddy, and I always loved that part. "Big Lo? Dat your 'lil' man?" his boys would yell as I ran across the dirt to greet my daddy. "Yeah, dat's Lil' Lo right there!" he would yell back and embrace me by picking me up and swinging me around. They would either call him Lopez (which was his middle name just like mine) or Big Lo, and I became Lil' Lo. Being called Lil' Lo always made me happy, and I knew it was a family thing. Not everyone had the esteemed privilege to do so, as it distinguished the true family from the others. Dad's outfits were always the same color and very bland. They would either be khaki, all blue, or sometimes orange. Looking back I wonder why I could never quite catch on to this being such a big clue in my life.

The year was 1986, and in retrospect, I was too young to catch in any of the missing links that were right there smacking me dead in the face. My direct memories growing up all consist of mostly females and my grandpa, "Billy" Ellis White. To be frank, he didn't take no sh*t. He was the one who taught me early on how to be a man and demand respect without having to bully others for it. It should come naturally. It wasn't my father; it was my grandfather (my mother's father), Billy White.

He was known all over the Southside of Richmond as the "fish man" or the "crab man' because he owned a local seafood spot that was the best in town called "Billy's Seafood." (My family claims this is where I began and developed my thirst to hustle because I was selling hot crab legs for 35 cents to the young'uns round the way.) He managed his own finances (with the help of my grandmother), kept his money in house, was a man's man, commanded authority and respect, and just an all-around real brother. Out of compassion for my mother, he even employed my father for a short period of time there (the memory is fuzzy to me). The thing is, he laid the foundation for most of the things that a father is supposed to do. Unfortunately, he died when I was 13 years old, and it crushed the family. Furthermore, it stopped me short of receiving my "how to be a man" and I still didn't have the right man for the job because he was always "away." I didn't find out until much later than 86' that he was incarcerated.

It was funny because I was so used to growing up without my daddy around that it wasn't odd for me even when other friends would ask me why my daddy wasn't around. I would say with my lil' chest out, "away at school." They were also young and naïve, so they didn't dispute it. Some of them had their fathers there with them, and some of their daddy's were "away" as well. That's how it was. Maybe if I didn't have anyone around it would have immediately affected me a little more; however, I had everyone around except him. I had my Aunt Valory (God bless her soul), my mother, my grandmother, my grandfather (God bless his soul), and plenty of friends. For those who grow up without a father or father figure in their lives, it doesn't really start hitting you until teenage years or higher. This is when it begins to mess with your mind. Some get quiet, some begin to lash out and take it to the streets, and some are like me and are simply lost but acting like everything is fine. Of course, I did the rebellion thing, but overall I just remember constantly having a head full of questions that couldn't seem to be answered by anyone. But I'm getting ahead of myself, because in 86' I was just going to hang out with my dad, the best dad in the world.

PAIN

I didn't know it at the time (and it hardly reflected on my face), but during my adolescence I harbored plenty of hate. Having the "best" dad in the world by day came with horrific pain by night. Secretly, I hated being a statistic. I hated that my mother had to struggle by herself to provide for me. As I got older, I hated that we had just one income in the house. I hated that we had to struggle. I hated the mystery. I hated the pain. I hated that society seemed to easily accept the high percentages of a father's absence in the family household. I hated my dad. Correction: I hated and loved my dad (and this was my ongoing "catch 22"). The mental pain of him being absent placed a scar on my heart… one that I thought could never be removed.

I remember plenty of the good times, and I guess it's even better that I really have to close my eyes and think hard to locate these feelings that I speak of, but they did exist. They existed for a long time. I felt pain because my mind and heart were seeking something for which at the time I didn't know what it was. It wasn't until later that I figured out just a few of the things that caused some of the pain from the disadvantage of not having the completeness of these qualities:

- Companionship from a male figure or role model
- The authority a father is supposed to possess and pass on to me
- The strength of a father that would combine with my own uniquely developed strengths
- Feeling needed by a father/parent, as well as being able to express the reciprocal need
- Simply having an available father to be able to watch/mimic his demeanor
- A father's wisdom and the different perspectives that he would bring versus my mother
- The way he was supposed to have made me better because of his positive characteristics rubbing off
- The inseparability of us two as we hang together, having folks see us as father/son combo

- The impact if I'd have had his stern correctness that would've helped me get back on the right path when I strayed while in my adolescence
- The learning of accountability
- The development of a genuine partnership
- The friendship that a father and son have the ability to share
- Lastly…..it is simply love. I was missing the authentic love of a father.

I was clueless, and I felt like only 50% instead of 100%. Sure, I was doing good and interacting as a general child, but overall I felt everything from anger, to emptiness, to confusion, to overall pain. Even during my teenage years, most couldn't tell it, but I was dealing with some deeply rooted issues regarding family. I've experienced family ups and family downs. Everything revolved around family- from love, to joy, to compassion, to loyalty, to frustration, and lastly, pain.

In retrospect to the past, I've realized that I can attribute some of the negative things that I did as a youth to not having a father figure in my life. Things like sleeping in mom's bed way longer than the average appropriate time (a clingy feeling towards my mother), severe behavioral problems in elementary school, whippings every day/mornings for not obeying my mother's instructions (sneaking stuff to school, mixed potions and daring people to drink it, and setting traps for my aunt inside her room), bullying people in elementary school, and much more. The troubles continued on through my teenage years. I did everything from shooting birds/animals with my BB gun (and burying them in my Grandma's backyard), to sitting on my front porch and shooting at school kids with it, to rolling around shooting out car windows in various neighborhoods with my friends, to shoplifting from numerous stores (no one knew).

Not having that structure or that sternness from a male/father figure in my life on a regular inadvertently brought on many outbursts and foul acts. In high school, I began to manipulate the minds of many girls throughout the years, and I'm sure this is highly due to not seeing a structured environment at home. I knew how to treat my mother, the females in my family, and even how to treat a woman (manners and all), but when it came to a female that I desired, I would eat them alive. I wasn't looking for the loving relationship that I witnessed my mother and father display as husband and wife, because I never saw it as they never had it.

I knew that I was very charming, witty, and charismatic, so I used what I had to the best of my abilities to establish a roster of females. This is not bragging at all, but in hindsight I see where it all originated and where the breakage in structure first began by not having a father. It is alarming when one analyzes the ongoing domino effect that not having a father figure in one's life can have over the years.

I still did the normal teenage stuff. I played in local Hoop-It-Up Games, took taekwondo (even received my black belt), went to the Boys Club, summer camp, learned to swim, played all sports and much more. Due to the fact that there was no father figure in the house, I began to attempt to make up for it by overachieving and acquiring many accomplishments. I guess this was so that I could say, "I don't need him." I earned everything from poetry scholarships, to countless trophies, book published, black belts in taekwondo, soccer championships, and more. I bought all of my cars myself and just made sure I overcompensated for the fact that the family was one short, but once again...that is in retrospect.

I know that as a man, people tend to force us to hide emotion. We seem "soft" and are immediately deemed as not being a "real" man. I have always been one to be able to express myself freely. A major contribution could be the fact that as a youth I was raised predominately by three women: my mother, grandmother, and aunt. With no major father figure around, I was taught how to be a man by three women (whom I will always love to death), my grandfather (until I was 13), and mainly my environment.

Most know that learning from the environment can have some bad side effects, so luckily those three women were my major influences, and they did all that they could to keep me grounded in righteousness. They gave my life its very first meaning, which was to succeed in all that I do. Success within can come with a very expensive price. This expensive cost can be love, loss, confusion, betrayal, and the list goes on. Sometimes that cost can even be family.

Sept. 8ᵗʰ, 1994

I remember my mother always being surrounded by family, but being alone regarding having a man around. I guess that was a good thing, being that so many single parents bring every Tom, Dick, and Harry around and wonder why their children view them in the light that they do. By this time, she had shared some information with me about my father, little by little. I had long ago found out that he had been in jail all these years and not in "school." That really hurt. I had asked her almost a million times on and off what he went in for, and she would hit me with the classic mother trying to protect someone line, "He was at the wrong place at the wrong time." At first, I would always accept it, but as I got a little older, I would question it more. I'd begin thinking to myself, "How is it the wrong time and he's always right at the wrong place to be, and right on time to get picked up by the police?" Then it went from that to me blurting out and verbally lunging out to my mom, "What does that mean???"

I couldn't recall in my memory's playback actually seeing him out of jail and around the house and the family, but maybe a few times. I could literally count on my hand how many times (and still have plenty room on my hand, too). There may have been many more, but as I stated, my mind just may have permanently blocked them out.

Yes, I spent a lot of time with him (many summers and more), but it wasn't the same. Ironically, I was very tight with his side of the family and used to spend very many days/nights over their side of town. They lived on the opposite side of town from ours-the West End. I even went to elementary school over there, right down the street from where his folks lived. I would take the bus from the Southside and get shipped all the way over to the West End to attend school there. I didn't know why, but I was just a kid so I had to go with the flow. Lopez's name hardly got mentioned unless they referenced me as his son, Lil'Lo. So once again, it was all love. No one was sad and somber. Not one day was I sitting in a dark corner wondering when my daddy was coming home. I was always surrounded by family love. It wasn't until I got older and my mind got to roaming that I began to get saddened (as well as angered) about this entire scenario.

As stated, time rolled on, and I got older. My mother began to give me more information, and also some of her actions had begun to show me she had moved on. She told me she divorced him awhile back (funny, I didn't remember a divorce, but then again I was a kid so I probably thought there was supposed to be a ceremony for that, just like a marriage), some time back in the 80's.

It was now the year 1994. My mother had a new boyfriend. They had just had a new son, and I was no longer an only child. My new brother was one year old now. This wasn't the typical case where the only child gets jealous of the new kid in the household. I had always loved kids, so when I had a brother to call my own, it was fun (thinking back, the only time I remember getting jealous at the thought was the moment my mother first told me she was having another child; I yelled out "wwwwhhhhyyyy?" But eventually I got over it). My brother and I were inseparable. I would watch him for my mother, play with him all the time, feed him his infant foods (snuck and tasted them, too), and be a big brother to him.

Ma and her boyfriend broke up. I liked him, but truthfully I didn't really care because I didn't want ma hanging out with any dudes anyway. I had a hard enough time fighting my friends from looking at her, because she looked so damn young. I knew she was attractive, but wouldn't dare say it. I'd drop one of them fools that I ran with if they said it in a disrespectful way. I would cut em' short by saying, "Chill, that's my mom, yo!" They had to respect that, but I still heard the whispers. I still saw the eyes jerk, and I still could smell the juvenile lust reeking on them. I didn't bring em' around much when I knew she was there. I know she paid them no attention, but those fools loved it when she would be nice to them. It used to piss me off. That was my early detection that I was overprotective of the women in my life.

Ma began to see the slow maturity in me as I was about to turn fourteen, and she decided to try to drop this bomb on me. It was three days after my 14th birthday, and she had decided to try her hand, so she sat me down to talk. Smiling at her, I was like "What now, ma?" She knew it was no laughing matter. She said, "Son, I have something very important to tell you. This may make you upset at me, sad, or feel nothing at all. I don't know, but I have to tell you.

I've been feeling so guilty regarding this, and I've already went to God about it. So now it's time I go to you."

I listened, as she proceeded to explain to me what sounded like Russian. She told me that the man who I knew my whole life as Daddy, the man who I heard referred to as "Lopez" and "Big Lo" wasn't my biological father. In a movie, this would be the part where all the jaws of those listening in the theatre would hit the floor simultaneously. I thought to myself, "She went to God for this?!?" Lopez isn't my father now? What? He was simply a stand-in (well, that's how I heard it in my mind). I quickly responded with a sharp "yeah, right" and stood up.

She signaled for me to sit down, and she went on to attempt to explain. She stated that she and my "real" father (at this time she hadn't mentioned his name) had just broken up, and afterwards she had found out she was pregnant. She didn't want to tell him and felt ashamed. Not too long after, she met Lopez. The smooth talker that he was, he knew she was pregnant, alone, and vulnerable. He told her, "Don't worry about it. I will take care of your son like he was my own."

Thus began their distorted relationship. None the wiser, they went on about their business and had everyone in the world thinking she was pregnant with his baby, when apparently that wasn't the case. She stated he even signed my birth certificate as my damn father! The thing is, she was telling this to a 14-year-old boy who loved his dad...in spite of.

When I love, I love hard, and it's hard to remove the love, so I wasn't trying to hear that nonsense that my mother was telling me. So what did I do? I got angry. I got irate, and I stormed off saying, "You're lying, that ain't true!" (So much for her efforts to have the truth revealed). I fought hard not to hear her, but deep down she caught my attention though...that inner fight just didn't seem to work all the time.

Trapped; Had to Fight

You always read or hear of people claiming to be terrified of being trapped inside some specific metaphoric realm ("walls") from which there's hardly any escape. In my eyes, the view was just the opposite. I felt trapped being in this open world, full of room to maneuver. I had a step-father who was *really* trapped inside those walls (and bars altogether.) I wanted to see him, but the truth was completely concealed from me that he was locked up in prison. I just wanted to get over the walls.

I remember the walls and the picnic table where we, as a family, would sit (you guessed it, visiting hours) and chat about sweet nothings. Those were the walls I knew of as a youth. My extended family packed up and moved to North Carolina when I was just a youngster. It hurt me not to be close to them. My favorite cousin who I had grown up with (within months apart age-wise) was gone. My outside walls were closing in on me. Sure we all would go visit them in Raleigh during the summer, and they would do likewise to Richmond for us, but it wasn't the same.

These were the beginnings of my many losses. Relationships, love, father to son, and so on. The fact that I knew that the information was actually there hurt the most. I would constantly ask my mother, "Where's daddy? Why did all my aunts, uncles, and cousins have to leave Richmond, and why can't they move back?" I had no siblings at the time, so they were all I had.

As I stated earlier, I was practically raised by three women. There weren't really any male figures, let alone role models around for me to learn the "essentials" from or to try and emulate. The only one who was around was my grandfather, Ellis ("Pa-Pa" is what I called him) White, and he died when I was thirteen [being trapped outside these particular walls of life were devastating, because these tragedies that I experienced were things that I sometimes saw coming, felt like I could prevent, and some caught me completely blindsided].

My mind's images of Pa-Pa are all of one main adjective: tough. He was very, very tough in my eyes (and the eyes of the entire Southside of Richmond city). His reputation represented the same thing, and no one I knew (or my parents knew either for that matter) would dare challenge it. I did have my fun times with him like tickling his feet until he took a swing at me and missed because he was too slow. There were plenty of times where I would sit in his favorite chair knowing that he was on the way downstairs (I was scared to death, but the daredevil within me was fearless).

We had our occasional happy times, but overall he was very frightening, and I knew my limits. When he was there, he was in fact, head of the household. That's one thing (from a visual standpoint) that I always saw and subconsciously learned. Sadly, my grandfather passed when I was thirteen, so my visual of that "tough" man stopped short. That was when things changed, along with the roles people play.

My immediate family was a small family of three. We had a single-family household system, single-income home, and my brother and I each have different fathers. My mother didn't have any financial support from a husband, and sometimes she had to get help from my aunt and grandmother. I was an only child for thirteen years, so each Christmas seemed as normal as everyone else's. It always seemed as if I had it made, but in actuality my mother just gave her all to ensure healthy holidays for me. It was never easy. Due to the constant struggle, I had to get my first job at the age of fourteen. It assisted with making a man out of me. At the age of sixteen, I bought my first car all by myself. I learned responsibility.

Another major influence on the struggle that I've had to deal with was taking one two major roles in my house-the brother and father. I am the older brother of my sibling, Devon (he's the youngest between the two of us), and I even played the father to him as well. Don't get it confused. He has a father, but I used to always tend to play a more active role in his life than his biological dad. I disciplined, supported and encouraged him, spared a shoulder whenever there was a problem, and contributed to many more things involved in his life than his "daddy" (let's hope things have changed by the time you read this).

One advantage of having a father in a young boy's life is that he can be there to teach him how to handle confrontations as a man. Learning these things as a boy can assist with the conversion of how to handle them as a man. One can combine the reasoning aspect and logic from his mother, and the confidence, heroics, bravery, and the removal of fear from his father. Many would say that, when faced with confrontation (in any form), we usually have two choices: run away or fight. No matter which one we may choose, they are both extremely hard to do. They are both hard to come to terms with as well.

Obviously, the easier one to choose would be to run away. When one chooses to run away, he or she is basically saying "I give up." What's hard to come to terms with is the fact that on the inside you now feel like a coward. Now, this is where you begin to stand in front of that mirror and let it all out! Afterwards, one usually begins to question himself like: "why did I do that?" or "What was I thinking?"

See, we've all run away from something in our lifetime. You could run away from inner confrontations with one's self, run from standing up to something that you've done, run from a consequence, a bully, etc. I've come to the conclusion that running away can only help one feel like he/she has survived for the brief moment. We all know that afterwards you have to figure out how to survive the next day, the next time, the next person, the next feeling, etc. Essentially, running away can really make life after that run harder for you than it ever was.

The fight inside of us tends to generate more energy than one could ever try to conjure up on his own. The adrenaline has to really be pumping sometimes for many to even feel the need to fight back. To fight is a very hard thing to do simply because of one very important point; you just might lose. Any human being on this earth can tell you that the one thing no one likes to do is lose (hence, the other option, to run away). The actual fight can either get one very excited to win or very scared by what would happen if they lose. If it's a physical fight, before it you're probably sizing up the competition. If it's an emotional fight, we're probably trying to foresee what consequences may come after it's over. Fighting is something that involves words such as pain, agony, strength, hurt, victory, defeat, apology, sorrow, sadness, stamina, faith, hope, and the list could go on forever. Something that involves so much can be enough to make someone think twice about doing it. It's scary either way it goes. Ah, but when you win the fight . . . oh, what a feeling you receive! Now, you've proved your point. You can't be stopped. You're the bigger man or woman, and you've conquered your current fears of failure . . . or have you? Once again, these things only last for the moment.

I can honestly say that I have two prime examples of a physical "run away or fight" scenario, both from my youth which during this time I had no father around. The first and second scene both take place in the same setting; however, these are two totally different situations. The first begins in an abandoned alley (or the "cut" as we used to call it) two streets over from my Grandmother's house. This area is where I spent the most of my youth growing up. It was the Southside of Richmond. It was also a very tough area back in the late 80's/early 90's.

This particular alley was the spot where everyone used to hang out and chill. As ironic as it may seem, it was also what my friends and I called the "danger zone!" We called it that because it was also the spot where all the fights, robberies, and chases occurred. Actually, this tiny area earned its title very well! In any event, my friend (who shall remain nameless) and I had to use this alley sometimes because it was a major shortcut to the shopping area called Southside Plaza. Everyone used this cut, this alley. We usually had it figured out precisely. We knew that you had to time it just right, and you'd make it through to the plaza.

This one particular day we didn't time it as precise as we thought. My friend and I were walking toward the cut, and we saw a few guys that we knew sitting out there. Now keep in mind, we knew them, but we didn't really know them (the late great Bernie Mac would understand that line!). Once we saw these guys sitting out there, my friend and I made the eye contact that you make where you don't have to say a word. You already know what to do. Still remaining calm (couldn't act like a punk out there), we continued to walk. The one guy closest (named Jamal) asked me for some money. I honestly told him that I only had ten dollars, which was for the rap CD that I was going to buy (you see, this guy Jamal kind of liked me, so he left me alone). He then proceeded to ask my friend the same question, but my friend gave him a flat out "no!" Instantly after hearing that, it, in turn, caused my heart to skip a beat! I was thinking, "What is he doing?" and "Why is it while I'm here?"

The guy said to him, "You think you can beat me, huh?" Guess what? My friend actually said "yeah!" From then, it was on! After Jamal heard the blatant disrespect, he felt he had been handed, he got heated. My friend said his piece and continued to walk through the cut; I followed. Out of nowhere, Jamal came flying at my friend and sucker punches him directly in the jaw (it looked painful)! He wrestled my friend to the ground (in the cut), and out of nowhere, three of his friends join in to assist him in this highly anticipated beat-down about to take place.

Now, I know you're all wondering, "Where were you in all of this?" Inside of my mind, body, heart, and soul, I was wondering the exact same thing! There I was witnessing an astonishing beat-down of one of my closest friends, and I was too fearful to help him. Was I mad at him, feeling like he wanted this fight to occur? Was I just scared of it, being the both of us getting jumped by these young thugs instead of just him? No matter the reason, I froze. I froze at crunch time, where it counted the most.

Fortunately for me (and unfortunately for me as well), he was getting beaten so badly that he never saw me freeze up on him. They beat him, stole his money, and ran off before he could do anything. I ran over there and became an actor, "Hey, you alright? I was fighting them, too. Who would've thought Jamal was going to do that?" Blah, blah, blah. He believed it, and we were still friends afterwards. The point of all this is that I, too, have run away before. It doesn't feel good at all. I felt like I wasn't a real friend. Like, he probably would've helped me, and I didn't do the same for him. I felt like the coward.

The second scene is indeed similar to the first, but the end results are totally different. It begins the same way...we were walking through the cut. This time we were very cautious and (to be quite honest and frank) scared. We didn't know what to think. We couldn't walk all the way around the neighborhood just to get to the Plaza. We just felt as if we had to at least attempt this again.

Well, just our luck, the boys were back. This time there were different faces, but the look in their eyes read the same agenda. Ah, but this time what they failed to realize was that I wasn't prepared to back down from anyone. Not today! However, my friend was terrified (flashbacks of the last whooping he received)! They must have received word about us coming, because they were ready, but so was I. We glanced at each other, nodded simultaneously, and took off running at top speed! They followed behind immediately, but had a hard time catching us.

Once I saw that they were gaining position on us, I stopped and picked up this gigantic stick. This stick may have been our lifesaver. You see, after the first time, I went and stashed this gigantic stick in the bushes so only I knew where it was (if you all could see me right now, I'm winking and nodding). As soon as the first gainer approached us and was within range, I swung that stick and clobbered him right across the head! That one blow was just enough to send him flying into the bushed where I stashed it. His friends came next, and I was more than prepared to swing at each. I told my friend to step back "I got them," and I swung this heavy stick in every way possible. I hit every last one of them at least once, leaving only one left.

This last one that was remaining was the brave one that pulled the stick out of my hand. Now I'm scared to death! Out of shear fear, I decided to throw a reckless punch in the direction of his face, and it actually connected. He collapsed head first on the ground. I kicked the stick out of his hand, and we ran right through the rest of the cut to the Plaza (who knows why we still felt the need to run when everyone was laid out on the ground, but we did).

That day was a major victory for us, but more importantly, for me! That was the day that I decided to fight, instead of run away. As stated before, it felt really good to win! There were many, many more days like that to come, but we now knew how we must face them. I had to learn from experience and my close peers versus a father figure to show me the right way how to handle these inner city scenarios.

The emotional fights (that we tend to encounter all too frequently) are much more complex than the physical ones. Mainly, because sometimes there are just too many battles to have to fight all at once! For instance, we may be dealing with some personal issue of ours (within one's self) and trying to juggle some of the family battles, as well as also trying to handle some friend issues, all while trying our absolute best to smile for the public. It's hard work! It can drain you and bring you down to your lowest form (if you let it) especially if all these things normally tend to run together and drag each other out. This is the time when you know you've got a serious fight on your hands. If you were to choose to run away from this one, it can only cause major problems in the future (far or near).

I would constantly run away from all of my emotional battles, especially those stemming from my fatherless bio. Those were usually the biggest fights, the ones that we'd begin to call on our heavenly Father for. The big battles, where we'd begin to schedule times to be able to discuss these serious issues with friends who we know we can trust. This is where we start to call on our mothers, fathers, sisters, brothers, and anyone who can possibly assist us with this situation. This is also a self-revealing time. This is the time where we begin to summon the inner fight within ourselves. Even after calling on everybody we know, at the end of the day we'll need to get through this by ourselves. This was the part where we summon up all the strength that we can muster. Take this strength, and distribute it out accordingly. Please, however, do not choose running away as an option. Speaking from experience, it will always come back to haunt you. Trust me. We all have before, but learning from that particular incident or situation is what strengthens us as well. I wish I would have known all of this when my mother was about to drop the bombshell on me. Maybe I would have been better prepared for the aftermath.

Nov. 8th, 1996

This time around I listened. It was a full two years later, and I was a very different young man. I had truly matured for my age, and that naïve state of mind that I was in was long gone. I was sixteen years old, and on my next to last lap of high school. I figured I could handle anything. I had finally turned my pathetic grades around, started focusing on what college I'd like to attend, and had a steady girlfriend. I guess mom decided it's time to try and drop this heavy, atomic bomb named *Biological Father* on me again.

Nov. 8th, 1996. It's crazy that I even remember the date. I want to say it was a Monday, but I'm not completely sure.
My whole world was about to change. No lie, this is literally the year that my entire world changed in a few powerful hours of conversation. My mother sat me down in her room, and she tried again. She had recognized where she went wrong from before. She tried to drop some heavy stuff on a kid barely 14. It wasn't going to work, because I wasn't ready then, but I am now.

She unplugged all the telephones in the house, so there wouldn't be any disturbances. Then she began to tell me about good ol' "dad-da" (as I used to call him). She explained to me from the beginning when they got married to where he is now and why he isn't with us. She told me some of the things he did to go to jail and why he stayed in there for so long. Before explaining everything to me, she started off by telling me that back then when she was with him, she was a weak-willed woman. She wasn't where she wanted to be spiritually and that he was a very persuasive man. After explaining the jail situation to me, I didn't believe her at first.

Before that incident I had always viewed my mother as someone who told the truth, but not anymore. She then explained to me that her reason for keeping a thing of this magnitude bottled up for so long is that she wanted me to be mature enough to handle what she was telling me. I don't even remember the divorce, but she told me that the divorce officially sealed it for him to never be able to come back into our lives. She continued to say that besides him going to jail, he wasn't the greatest husband either! He had cheated a few times, and he had also beaten on her before. She must have mumbled that part, because I know I would have went off if I had caught wind of the latter information that she had just exposed to me.

She backed up and went over the original information from two years before. All too familiar, I listened as she recited the news that I had thought I'd purposely blocked out. Again, she stated that she and my "real" father had just broken up, and afterwards she had found out she was pregnant. She didn't want to tell him and felt ashamed. Not too long after, she met Lopez. The smooth talker that he was, he knew she was pregnant, alone, and vulnerable. He told her, "Don't worry about it. I will take care of your son like he was my own." Yeah, right. Their relationship prospered temporarily, while her now ex was none the wiser. He moved on to the next one.

She told me that my biological father's name was Chris- Chris Anderson to be exact. She reminded me that she tried to tell me all of this two years ago, but I had stormed out in an "understandable" rage. "Damn right I did" I thought to myself. "Look at this mess you're telling me, ma." I'm glad she couldn't read my thoughts. I kept listening attentively as she continued to pour out the guilty truth that dwelled in her heart for 16 years. She was a saved woman. I had watched her read that Bible faithfully and evolve, so I knew this had been severely bothering her. There are billions of other women out there who would take this sort of thing to the grave with them (and they should be shot for such a thing), so I think I listened partly also because I secretly commended her for that (but mainly intrigued at the information being presented on a dreary platter).

By the age of sixteen, I had developed a love/hate feeling for my father, Mr. Lopez (not Lopez as of Spanish decent, it was just his middle name. I got teased for years). The hate was winning by a long shot, and the love had been pushed way down to a place that would be very hard to find. I knew it was still there, but I knew what was prevalent-the hate. The hate had simply formed over the years from not being able to see my father.

I had heard all of the "I love yous" I needed to here, and I just wanted him around. I didn't care that they were divorced. I just wanted him around. I wanted some answers, and I got none. I didn't have a physical body to look at and examine our similar qualities. I didn't have a man to project my future aspirations after, a man to show me how to throw that special one, two punch, ride a bike like him, fix the kitchen sink, or fix a flat. I didn't have a man named "Daddy" that was around for me to try to prove I'm a man, too. I always had to prove it to mom, grandma, and my peers. I remember on numerous occasions as a youngster going to visit him and sitting on his knee. He'd tell me "You know I love you right? And I'm going to be home soon." With a smile he said this. On plenty nights, I laid up replaying that line…afterwards I said "F you daddy; I hope you never get out of prison."

That was why I had originally hated him, but there were more reasons why I began to want him dead. In my eyes, it was due to him that all during my high school years I was so confused about my own makeup. It was like once I found out the truth about my biological father, everything in life went blank for me. I wanted to disown all that I knew not to be blood. I felt tricked. I felt short-handed and disadvantaged. I looked at God, I looked at my mother, I looked at Lopez, and I looked at the stranger now known as Chris as all being in on some secret joke on me.

I was so hurt, but more confused than anything. I held plenty in after fully receiving this news and accepting it as truth. I began to wear a mask, a false face for many. I knew I still had to be me to many, so I played my role as the show doesn't stop because one person has a life-changing revelation revealed to them. I knew that; however, now, if I didn't already struggle with being a man due to having no male in the house, I knew that I would surely struggle upon knowing my biological father isn't who I thought he was.

I struggled for years upon years, too. I used to put it at the back of my mind and not mention it for months. Then it would re-surface, and I'd go into a mental slump at times. Who could I talk to about it? I couldn't go to my mother because whenever we attempted to discuss this issue, I'd get enraged, and she'd feel guilty. We'd both just end up walking away. No one else knew, so I had no alternatives; I was caught between a rock and a hard place.

I wasn't living right, and God and I weren't on the best of terms in my eyes. I didn't even attempt to go to Him, though I was in church faithfully every Sunday. My church (which was Baptist at the time) didn't really teach holy living, just that no matter what you may do, Jesus saves, etc. So I used to be in there every Sunday, but living like a lil' devil throughout the week (like many others in there that I knew). I felt that I couldn't' go to God with that mentality. The ongoing pain was just too much at times. I was all messed up.

As my mother kept pouring out her heart, she then said something that struck a vital nerve in my body. She said that the man formally known to me as "Dad" had at times sporadically beaten her. As stated, I must've missed it the first time she slid it in the conversation, because I yelled out "What!?!"

"He had beat me," she said with her head hanging down in shame.

"Why'd you let him do that!?!" I bellowed, now standing, ready to kill that fool.

She said that she used to always try to fight him off of her, but he was too strong. She said this used to happen when I was very young, as an infant/toddler I'm guessing. I'm guessing, because I don't remember that fool even being around like that, but sometimes our memories as a small child get erased. Well, thank God for that notion, because what she told me next tipped the iceberg. It pushed me (as well as any love that I had remaining) over the edge. The ledge was no more.

Whenever I tell new people who enter my life this story, I always refer to this part, as "the scene." Ma painted me a graphic depiction of a time where she states she "almost lost her life." She said that I didn't even know it, but I saved her life just by being there. "As an infant, I saved a life?" I wondered, as I listened further.

My mother had a way with depicting stories (I later realized that my father does as well, and that's why I now tell them so descriptively). Not only would she cry, express her anger, guilt, pity, and all other emotions, but she would make you feel it. She would bring you right there in that very same room that she was in when it all took place. She took me there. It was a place where I didn't want to be, though I hadn't even been there before. Never have I witnessed domestic violence, not then and not now. Little did I know, she knew of it firsthand from the man who I foolishly called "Daddy" for 16 years.

Before getting to "the scene," she began describing the random yet frequent beatings that she received whenever he was home long enough to raise his pathetic fist. Without any real specific information given, she explained that he used to hit her off and on. These were on the rare occasions that he'd be home. I was thinking to myself, they must have done an excellent job of keeping these things hidden because I don't remember a thing ever happening while growing up there.

I remember all of our homes though. Born in Southside, as well as having my mother born and raised in the Southside in the early 80's, we began living in these "hood" apartments, called "Stonybrook". Then we moved to Castlewood Road in Southside, which wasn't too much better, but at least we had a house (later, it became known around the way as "dead man's row").

My mother wasn't a person to let an environment or situation ever hold her down, so she found a way to move clean across town to Chesterfield County. I remember all the way up to my high school times that I couldn't stand it out there in the county. I hated the neighborhood, some of the people, and always used to beg my mother to take me and leave me at my grandmother's house back in Southside. She would oblige me, and I found my way back to Southside every day. I even stayed there for full weekends on in. She had what she wanted, which was to get us out of those ragged areas filled with crime and establish a real home for her family. I didn't recall seeing Lopez at any of these homes (maybe I blocked it out of my mental imagery).

It wasn't until sometime in high school that my mother told me I needed to start staying in our own neighborhood instead of constantly running back and forth to Southside. This time I listened. It was getting very bad around my grandmother's way. If I probably had continued running with the guys I was running with, I would have been where they are now, which is dead or in jail with plenty of street scars to show. I thank God for a praying mother and a determined mother.

Apparently, I was just finding out that she had Lopez still showing his face around these various homes, and most importantly, placing hands on my one and only mother. After hearing about that, I was too through with him. My love switched over so fast, you'd think I never had it. No one puts their hands on my mother. No one. He was no exception because I called him "Daddy," and I wanted to make him pay, just as I would if I found out that another did so. Ma wouldn't have it. She just made me simmer down as she continued.

She then backtracked to my birth certificate. She explained that she wanted to leave it blank, but he "insisted" that he sign it with his name as my biological father. This fool even had the audacity to name ME with his same name, as if I'm following behind him! As if we shared the same blood! As if he was ever a damn father to me! As if! I was named as Vincent Lopez Mapp III on September 5, 1980 in Richmond Memorial Hospital on the Southside by a false father, and my mother sat by and watched it happen. That hurt my soul.

Little did I know that it wasn't simply her sitting by in idle as he made these types of moves. There were serious threats (some even backed up with physical force) made on her life, MY life, and much more. At that time, I guess she felt very helpless and fearful, so she compromised her own judgment, faith, and rearing to save those whom he mentioned. He made her keep this "secret," and she most certainly did. No one knew or was the wiser of such a secret. No one knew that Lopez wasn't really my biological father, not a soul on his side or my mother's side. Hell, I didn't even know until the age of sixteen!

"That woman sure can keep a secret," I thought to myself as I stared at my mother while she dropped numerous tears to the floor, "and he was in jail so there was no one to really listen to him even if he wanted to tell someone." But, he never wanted to tell; he was going to take this one to the grave, that sneaky bastard! I sure am glad that God placed an active conscience in my mother's head to be able to push her to expose this dreadful truth about my father and life. Shoot, I had the right to know years ago, not at the age of sixteen and not like this!

I interrupted her and said, "Alright, ma, I get it, I get it; I don't wanna hear no more."

She said, "Ok, but I do have to tell you about when he almost killed me."

"Here we go," I murmured as I just buried my head in my chest ...

Childhood Message

During my adolescence, I remember I used to always wonder the true definition of a man. Well, the *American Heritage Dictionary* defines it as "a male human being having qualities considered characteristics of manhood." The definition hasn't changed at all, but life sure can re-define it. If that direct definition of a man is in fact that, then the man I used to call "father" definitely doesn't fit anywhere within the means of that category.

I always thought that my ideas of being a man would be formed from a father figure, but the actions of this guy Lopez that I was calling "Da-Da" since my toddler years ended up affecting my gender identities by him portraying something other than what he told me. He told me what a man should be and how one should act (key word "told"). He would use the term "real" to show the distinction between the fathers of the family. He would always give it to me straightforward. He always told me that any man with a fully functioning sex organ could impregnate a woman and become a father, but the real man he had referred to earlier was the one who actually takes good care of their kids and provides for his family.

That is a good philosophy to tell someone, but I also believe if you give someone that type of message, you should live by it also.

Such a childhood message can come from just observing. I truly can see now that observation is knowledge. Lopez never proved to me that he can live up to everything that he used to preach to me about as a youth. All of my observations of him weren't the things that were needed to properly teach a child.

While preaching his personal message, what he failed to mention was that he was in and out of jail. He was in and out of jail most of my entire childhood for all types of different things, and he never had the guts to tell me. He would preach to me when he came home on occasion, or at times he would even do it directly from the jails. I guess he felt like he needed to teach his son something important; and having his son seeing him in jail wasn't doing the trick. This was totally wrong because, in actuality, it was doing the trick very well.

Of course, now I know that he was in the wrong, but at the time everything he said to me was correct in my eyes. I actually used to look at him as the perfect father at times (when I was clueless), and later as my eyes opened, I began to see through the cluelessness, confusion, and hurt. I can admit that when he came home we had some good times, but that doesn't hide the fact that he was a terrible father to me, and worse, caused ongoing pain to begin formation inside of my heart as a young boy.

Another reason I openly believed all of his lies and deceptive words was because I knew my mother did. So, in turn, I did as well. My mother would take me to visit him in jail. I'd see him and would just start playing with him outside and enjoying myself out in the open. It wasn't to my knowledge that it was his visiting hours and that's why he had so much freedom to roam around. I didn't blame my mother. Once I found out later that she didn't just do that on her own but that he made her do it; it was curtains for him.

He made her lie to me about everything, even threatened her! He would tell her to keep him being in jail a secret. He felt that it would ruin our "wonderful" relationship that we had. Boy, was he right! Though him finding out that he was so right didn't come into play until the future. He would make my mother tell me all types of lies just to keep that close bond of ours. We would go see him every week. It became so routine that I didn't even think about it. I would just get up and go.

My idea/definition of a man is a little bit different. It is that a man must at all times support his family, be a loving and caring husband and Christian, abide by the law, and uphold to each part that he has vowed to serve. From my childhood to my current state, his moves affected my current moves today. I would tell any fathers out there to make sure that their words completely match their actions, because their sons are definitely watching, listening, learning, and eager to follow. Luckily, I had three wonderful women (grandmother, aunt, and mother) to guide me in the right direction and not allow this negativity to hinder my path to excellence (especially the physical abuse towards a woman).

*_**Matthew 23:9** "And call no man your father upon the earth: for one is your father, which is in Heaven."_ *

"The Scene"

"He came home and came right at me," she said, as she looked straight into my pupils. I was nervous as I listened. My hands shook uncontrollably as I followed along and hung on to each verb and adjective spoken. Here she was describing how the man that I always knew as my father was trying to kill her. She said he came home and came directly at her, as if he had a bone to pick with her all day long. She swore up and down that she didn't do anything to him, hadn't even seen him all day, and he just lunged at her after coming in the house.

What disturbed me greatly was when she said that I was an infant sitting right there on the couch (somewhere in between the age of 12-18 months). She said that at first I was just sitting there sort of staring aimlessly, but then as the yelling and screaming got more intense, I began to cry…then howl…then it got to that silent cry where you just have your mouth wide open but no sound is coming out, nor are there any more tears flowing. I guess I was all cried out.

She said they were both struggling in the living room at first, but then he overpowered her and threw her onto the stairs that led upstairs. These were the very same stairs that I've traveled up and downward on for years, and the very same stairs that she still uses to this very day. "I'm going to kill you're a*s!!" he snarled and grumbled, all while struggling to position himself perfectly so that he could do just that.

My mother is a very strong woman physically (and emotionally), but I could begin to feel that this was enough to break the best of them. She began to cry uncontrollably as she continued. Sniffling, she said that Lopez had finally begun to cut off her air supply, and she felt herself getting dizzy. She felt herself struggling less because she no longer had the energy to fight him. All she had was her God, her wit, and her words. Apparently, it was all that she really needed.

As she felt her last breaths being taken away from her, she mustered up all of her inner strength to be able to say to him, "So, you're going to kill me right in front of your son? Is this really how it's going to end, with him watching his father strangle his mother?"

She lifted her head from inside her hands, wiped her tears, and said to me: "Lil' Lo, it could only be God that saved me, because after I said that he turned around and looked at you...you looked at him (not crying anymore)...and once you two made eye contact, he simply let me go. It was just that easy for him." Then she began bawling again.

"Damn, ma," was all I could muster up my vocal chords to say (even though my mind, heart, and soul was thanking God for divine intervention yet again).

High School Graduation

It was my mother's 43rd birthday, June 15th, 1998, and coincidentally, I was also having my high school graduation on that very same day. She was oh so proud. She was hilarious, as she strutted herself all around the house earlier that day. I couldn't laugh though, because I was doing the same. This was my friggin high school graduation, and with all that I had been through, I was going to rejoice for sure! I was 17 years old, just recently accepted into the school of my choice (Norfolk State University), and finally getting the hell out of Richmond. Sure I was excited. Little did I know the total shocker that lie ahead.

I remember still remaining tight with a few of my family members on my now ex-Dad's side (I guess he could have been considered a "step-father," but I wasn't having it). After all, we all had grown up together and were very tight. Even after all of this newly found information, I didn't want to just abandon them like that because they weren't considered my "blood" any longer. I can't lie though. When I first found out about Lopez not being my father, I wanted to distance myself from his entire side of the family for a good minute. I had nothing against them, but it was just that everything felt fabricated to me after hearing the news.

It felt like all of the love given, the caring received, the numerous babysitters I had, the constant playing outside, many overnight stays and all didn't matter anymore because I felt that way. I also wanted to tell the world, but out of respect for my mother's personal wishes, I kept my mouth shut to everyone. Well, to almost everyone. I told my then girlfriend at the time and my best friend, but I absolutely told no one on Lopez's side. In their eyes, everything was still the same.

I decided to invite my closest cousin on his side, and in turn, told them to bring my grandmother whom I called "Nanny". Sure, with my recently found news, she wasn't really my grandmother by blood, but I had to let certain things slide. That woman helped raise me like my grandmother on my mother's side did. She watched over me many nights, took care of me, shielded me from all of the dangers that lurked in their area of the West End, and much more. No, I couldn't ever disown her, so I had to have her there.

Graduation day was the most exciting day of my seventeen-year-old life. I was snapping pictures all day long and just laughing and joking with all of my high school friends. It was going to be at the Richmond Coliseum. I remember feeling like it was super important because it was going to be there. This was the same place that all the big rap/R&B stars came to perform.

During graduation, I could hardly contain myself in my chair. We had to listen to those same old boring speeches that come along with graduation, and my friends and I were just sitting together cracking jokes and acting goofy. Everyone was just anxious to walk across that infamous stage and do something to make people laugh. We lined up on the right side and began marching. I was in line with those that had the last name beginning with "M," so I was kind of in the middle section. As I inched closer and closer, I let my eyes scour the room until I could spot my mother, grandmother, little brother, and best friend. I didn't even think to look for my cousin and them from Lopez's side. Once I spotted them, everything was all good. I threw my hands up in the air to them and marched forward. Closer and closer I came to the stage.

Finally, 'Vincent Lopez Mapp III" they spoke into the microphone. As I heard my name echo throughout the Coliseum, I eagerly stepped up on stage. I paused and put my left hand up, circled it like the wrestlers would do, and put it to my left ear in hopes of hearing my crowd/fans howling for me. I wanted to hear my name, and I heard it. So I skipped on across that stage and got my diploma. I shook the hand of the principal and two other faculty members, paused for a close up picture, pointed up to my family in the crowd with a "we made it' type gesture, and danced on down off of the stage. Yes, it was a glorious evening!

Afterwards, all of the graduates were supposed to meet and greet their guest's right outside of the Coliseum, and that's where I headed. I walked around the Coliseum for a few minutes and couldn't locate anyone. The Coliseum was circular, and once I was almost completely around it, I finally bumped into my mother and family.

"Awwwwwwww c'mere Lil'Looooooo!" my mother whined with tears already running down her face, as she ran to hug me.

I embraced her and my little brother tightly, and when I let go, my best friend came right after to pound me up and congratulate me for my accomplishment. My best friend had to leave after a while, so my mother, brother, and I began to walk back around the Coliseum again.

All too excitedly I was speed walking ahead, looking around trying to see who all was there, when I hear 'Heeeey man, congratulations!" This was an all too familiar voice to me. It was the voice of a man, which just the mere thought of him made me cringe.

It was Lopez. "I thought yo' a*s was in jail," I thought to myself, as I stopped dead in my tracks and stared him down. He still looked just as I pictured him to look. I hadn't seen him in a long while, but sure enough, it was him. He had a half beard flowing from his sideburn connecting to the bottom of his chin. He was short in stature, brown skinned, and had a low cut, grinning real hard.

After hearing from my mother what he did to her, I had convinced myself that the next time I saw him I was going to put my foot in his a*s, but for some strange reason I didn't have the instant urge to do so. I was more so shocked that he was out, and that he even had the audacity to show up at my graduation like he played some intricate part in it. He just stood there, and so did I.

I felt my mother's presence brush up against me from behind, but I didn't turn around. I wanted to stare this no-good, worthless bastard down without a blink. I wanted him to make some type of move on me (even though he had no reason to be mad at me; he didn't even know that I knew the "secret"), but he didn't.

He reached out and embraced me with a hug and while inside his hug, I lay there lifeless and dormant. He let go after realizing that I wasn't going to hug him back. He then reached out and tried to "dap me up," but I didn't put out my hand. I smacked his down. I smacked his down and demanded, "What are you doing here?" My mother then interfered and said, "Lil' Lo, don't act that way. He came here to congratulate you."

I said, "Whatever" and stormed off. He had officially ruined my graduation just that easily. I was disgusted with him.

NSU Junior Year 2001

The year was 1999, and it was my sophomore year at Norfolk State. To say that I was loving life at the time would have been an understatement. The numerous parties, step shows, frat cookouts, pep rallies, talent shows, homecomings, concerts, midnight madness basketball games, and the female to male ratio of 12:1!! I was too through; I loved my HBCU with a passion. I had moved from the ghetto dormitory named Scott Hall that I was living in to a nicer dorm on the other side of the school-Charles Smith dormitory.

My best college buddy at the time had moved with me, and we were very close. We went through the school year and throughout all of the excitement, I knew I had some dark days ahead of me. I had to tell my roommate because we were close, though I knew he would be disappointed in me. He didn't know of my endeavors that I'd encountered back at home in Richmond, nor did he know about the consequences that I was about to have to face.

During the summer that had just passed, I was working at Staples back at home in Richmond and was having a beef with some local knuckleheads who used to hang around that way where my job was. They kept leaning on my car and hanging around my car daily. So, one day I approached them and told them to choose another car because that was my car. We argued a bit but nothing transpired.

The very next day I was at work, and during my lunch break I went outside to go to my car and found that the tires had been slashed along with a crack in the window. I immediately knew who it was, and I was so heated. When I got off of work, I didn't rush to my car; I waited around. I waited real late, long after my 5pm shift had ended.

When I saw the one guy out of the crew who was doing the most popping off at the mouth at me that day, I eased up on him. I did it so smooth that I caught him completed off guard. As soon as he finally saw who I was, he instantly got thumped in the mouth! Swiftly, I moved, before he could either swing back or even call his boys for assistance. I caught him with a sharp knee to the stomach, and he slid down on the car nearest to him. But I wasn't finished yet.

They had tried to punk me, as well as one of them had damaged my new car. Since he was there at the time, he had to pay. Once I looked down and saw him lying there slumped, I took the opportunity to kick him in the face. That was the final blow that I needed to feel vindicated. After that last kick, I vanished; however, even when I got out of sight and safely at home, I secretly yearned for more.

I took off the next day to let some of the drama simmer, but I wasn't done with them. I had a final plan to finish them off and make sure they never F'd with Vincent ever again (nor my car). I had watched and realized that the folks in their crew parked their cars around the side of my job. So, late that next night I went and slashed each of their individual tires on their nice whips and even took the available cd books that were exposed in one of the convertibles. I used my exactor knife that I use to keep with me. I felt vindicated finally, and afterwards I dipped off the scene. As you can probably tell, I wasn't acting like I had an ounce of holiness in me during this period.

No later than the next week, late in the wee hours of the morning, I received a strange phone call. It was from a police officer. I thought it was a prank call, but quickly realized that it was serious. I immediately got so nervous, but tried to act hard. He asked me did I know anything about any tire slashing going on in that area where I worked; I denied everything.

What scared me the most was when he apparently got tired of my games and came right out and said, "Either you can come to the station so we can talk about this, or I can send a squad car to your house to get you?" "Brrr," I said to myself (in my Tim the Tool Man voice from the hit show *Home Improvement*). Being that it was almost three in the morning and I didn't want my mother knowing anything, I chose to sneak out and drive to meet this cop. Nervous as I was, I drove towards him following the directions he gave me.

I ended up deep in Chesterfield at the police station around 3:20a all by myself. Growing up, most of us kids are taught by others around the way to never talk to cops, snitch, show fear, etc. I was trying to roll with that, but it isn't the same when you're all alone in front of one and you know you did the crime (nor did I know the severity of the crime).

He explained that the charges weren't just slashing a tire, but it was several counts of vandalism, grand theft larceny (from the stolen cds totally over $500), and that it faced mandatory jail time. My heart dropped. It was hard to continue lying to him, playing dumb, and acting tough when he mentioned that, but more so when he said, "Plus, we have the tape from the parking lot, and I know it was you Mr. Mapp." My jaw dropped. In all of my planning, I never thought about them having a security camera rolling on the parking lot, but it made perfect sense. Then my mind went to the brutal fight scene that I started and finished, and I got even more petrified. I was sitting there listening to see when he was going to pull out the big gun and tell me I also have an assault charge...but he never did. He wanted a confession from Mr. Mapp III confirming the tire slashing that he had already seen me doing. In my head I weighed my options, and they were very limited. Here I was being called Mr. Mapp just like sorry-a*s Lopez and about to be jailed just like sorry-a*s Lopez. Maybe he had rubbed off on me more than I knew.

I decided to confess. I just didn't want my mother involved, so I was willing to do anything not to have her wiser. He told me if I confessed he would let me go home that night and just give me a pre-trial date. If I didn't, he would have to book me, and I'd sit in jail. Needless to say, I confessed.

In my confession, I still lied a bit about how many of their cars I slashed. I made it my case to explain why I did it and what they had done to my car. It didn't work. He still charged me with six counts of vandalism and grand theft larceny, but I got to go back home that night. I sat up all night and pondered how I was going to get myself out of the mess that I was in.

Over the next few weeks, I told no one. I didn't get a lawyer, nor did I tell my mother; I just let it sit as if nothing happened. I went to the pre-trial by myself and plead guilty. When the real trial came up, I went in there with my mother and newly-hired lawyer accompanying me. I had literally told my mother just two weeks before the trial, and she laid me out for it all; however, I was still her son, so she got me a lawyer.

During my trial, my lawyer and I described how I was getting good grades at NSU, working, in church, didn't have a criminal record, etc. The judge still gave this young black man 30 days with 27 suspended. I didn't comprehend the time. When he gave the sentence out, my lawyer looked at me and gestured to me as if saying that it was a good sentence or some sort of victory. I looked back at him like, "fool, I ain't doing no damn jail time!" Instead, I said something to the effect of, "If he's saying I have to do some jail time, that's out of the question!"

The lawyer began reasoning with me stating that most people would get more time and trying to get me to understand, but I just couldn't understand that I had to sit in a cell. I asked the judge was there anyway I could avoid jail time, but he said there wasn't. He said that I was lucky to get the grand larceny charge removed on account of the owner of the car didn't show up to trial and I returned the cds. Most people would do the full 30 days, but he saw potential in me by being in college. He then offered me to do the days on a weekend, and I could pick the weekend. It would either be on my Thanksgiving or Christmas break from college. I chose turkey day. I couldn't see myself locked up around Christmastime.

During the fall semester was when I told my roommate and also when I had to complete my time. He was severely devastated that I would do such a thing, as well as the fact that his boy had to do some jail time. Thanksgiving break rolled around, and everyone was excited except me. The judge allowed me to do my weekend term in

Richmond versus Norfolk, so when I got home that Friday evening I was taken straight to the Chesterfield jail by my mother. She dropped me off after praying with me. Then she vanished, and it was just me.

The first person who entered my mind as I walked through those jail bars and as they closed on me was Lopez. I wondered how I had gotten myself into this mess, and how the hell did I end up on his same track. Sure it was merely a weekend versus his many years, but some say that is how it starts. I was determined to let it end there.

I remember not taking a shower all weekend. I remember doing a crazy amount of push-ups because that's what I thought you were supposed to do in there. I remember playing Spades, Deuces, Crazy 8's, and all of those other oldie but goodie card games, with all of the other criminals in there. We all looked different, but we were all just alike-locked up. I remember my top bunk bed was right below the ceiling light, so it was mega-hard to go to sleep at night staring at a bright rectangular light.

I remember hardly eating, because the food tasted like waste management recycled it, put it in the microwave and served it to us. Everyone else locked in with me would always get excited when I would offer to give my food away; I didn't care. I remember the old-timers would sit me down for what seemed like eons and tell me how much I didn't belong in there and that I need to get out and finish school. There was a lot that I remembered and will still remember to this day.

I wrote this while locked in there

"Weekend Term"

No man could explain (the unbearable pain I felt (
When the judge's gavel hit the wood (
Those were the cards that were dealt (
In front of him, nervously I stood (
Thinking, 'if I could rewind time, I would... (
But now I'm doomed' (
Simply stuck, with my fate in the mind of one man
in that cold room (
Hit with a short stint of jail time (
At a loss for words, not speaking (
Nineteen years of age (
Giving the system his precious time for one dreaded
weekend (
Around turkey day is when I would creep in (
Friday at six p.m. (
Sunday at six is when I was scheduled to leave (
Someone whispers for God to pray for young V. (
Fear filled and consumed his heart (
His mind clogged with nothing but negative thoughts (
This must be the lesson, I should've been taught (
But overlooked it (
Now, simply a stranger in a small room (

Where everyone is looking/
Trying to decipher my life's resume/
Asking so many questions/
Like, "how long is your stay?"/
I'm trying so hard, just to stay to myself/
Tossed my clothes up on the top shelf/
Jumped up on my bunk/
Closed my eyes, and just began to pray for my own
health/
Folks of all shapes, ages, sizes, and races/
Fighting over specific spaces/
Playing cards, throwing up aces/
I put up a good front/
Like I'm as real as they come/
Kept a frown on my face/
Doing consecutive push-ups, counting by ones/
I just couldn't believe what I had slowly become/
A statistic to society/ Should I take it and run?/
Or make a change and not succumb/
Try to make the darkest place enjoyable and fun?/
I decided to leave it as what it is/
Miserable and depressing/
Insomnia, no sleeping at night/
Horrible meals I'm slowly digesting/

Dealing with the thousands of thoughts inside my head/
The roughness of that used bed/
Protecting every single body part/
From my head, to my legs/
To God I begged/ Sunday reaches me quick/
Or at least an answer to my prayer beat Sunday to it/
My body felt numb inside of that bottomless pit/
Named jail, prison/ Rather it renamed hell behind bars/
Oh, the pain, the emotional scars/
This place, where everything is filthy/
From the people, down to the soap bars/
Many thoughts tempted me/
But, I discerned and rationalized each decision/
My natural intuition told me/
I simply didn't belong in that prison/
Ironically, some folks were friendly/
Some appeared as future enemies/
I stayed quiet/
& let no one attempt to befriend me/
Took no showers/
From fear of several programs/movies seen on TV/

When Sunday finally came/
On that exit, my eyes were aimed/
The cell opened slowly, so anxious was I to run/
Shamed, & kept this secret buried deeply within me/
No words of it have come.....until now.

Written by: Mr. Vincent Ellis White ©2001

I did my weekend. I thugged it out. Nothing happened to me, and on Sunday evening at 6pm (which matched the time I went in on that Friday), I came home. When they allowed me to walk up out of that huge jail cell and I got outside and saw my mother waiting for me, it felt like boulders being released off of my shoulders. I did it, it was over, and now I could get back to school and put it all behind me, because I definitely learned a valuable lesson while being locked up with all those criminals, drunks, thieves, and more. I couldn't stand jail or prison, and I'd never set foot back inside a cell ever again. I didn't want to do anything that would have someone associate me with the likes of Lopez.

NSU Junior Year '01 is what I called my breakout year. It was the year that I turned 21, the year I had obtained my first apartment ever (I was finally off campus), and the year that I finally got up the gall to change my last name. This thing with my real dad and my false dad had still been bothering me off and on. Sometimes I would completely forget about it, and other times I'd sit and ponder about it, get very anger at all the parties involved, or cry out of confusion. Only those who may have gone through life only to find out someone so dear and/or close to their heart isn't their father and that the real one is somewhere out there but you have no clue as to his whereabouts can know this feeling and understand this mixing of emotions that never seem to end.

I had only told a handful of people by now, and even in the midst of all the fun that I was having at Norfolk State, I still felt empty inside. I felt like I didn't know who I was. I was living a lie. It was different when I didn't know that I was living a lie, but I had now known since I was sixteen years old, yet I was still answering to a false last name. I would still raise my hand when my last name was called. I would still sign my last name Mapp III in cursive, and it was driving me insane.

What made it worse was that my mother had still kept the last name Mapp, even though they had been divorced since the 80's. Whenever I had begged and pleaded with her to change it, she always said "no". She said that she would have too much stuff to change over and that it wasn't a big deal to her, but it was like a slap in the face to me and a very big deal. We argued several times about it, but she wouldn't budge, so I made it my purpose to budge.

While in Norfolk, I inquired with the courts and City Hall downtown about the procedure to do a name change. I had no idea how simple it was to change one's name. It was just a little form that I had to fill out, provide a birth certificate, social security card, pay $10 or so, and it was changed. I had thought this move out for many months and years, but it was this year that I knew I had to take action. My mother was still holding on to that wretched last name, and I couldn't bear to continue to carry it anymore.

I had only one last name option in mind-White. It was for numerous reasons. My mother's original last name was White, my grandmother's was as well, and my grandfather (with whom I was so close to) Ellis "Billy" who passed away when I was 13 had also carried that last name. His first name was Ellis, his last name was White, and he was a black man in my family who demanded respect. There were also many other first cousins in my family who all carried the middle name Ellis and last name White. So I decided to switch my name from Vincent Lopez Mapp III to Vincent Ellis White. After writing it on the documents to turn in to the courts at City Hall in downtown Norfolk, after a few business days I became a new man. It was just that easy.

I felt some of the confusion leave me, even though no new information had been found. I had made a list of all the businesses, people and more that I had to alert of the change, and I did so. I told everyone. I sent out copy after copy of my name change documents to everyone from banks, to my school, to my job, and many more. I was a completely newly renewed person in my mind, and when I told my mother I believe she was relieved. She was more so relieved because she knew how much it meant to me to have such a thing done.

Of course, I got the millions of questions as to why I changed it, and I told many different answers. To some it was sort of a dedication to my grandfather, and some because I didn't ever really know my father, but really it was a combination of all those along with the fact that the White's were the only family with whom I knew without a doubt that I shared true blood with. It wasn't like I would go change it to Anderson, because I didn't know that man. All I had was a name with no face or description.

It didn't matter how many people asked me about the name switch. I had now shed off the last bitter piece of anything associated with Lopez or Mapp, and I felt refreshed. I had finally shed the last name of the man who lied and hid the truth from me, the man who was never there for me, the man who dared to put his hands on my mother, the man who was jailed for most of my entire life, the man I hated for years. I was back to being a White, which is who I grew up with on a daily basis for my entire life anyway.

I remember feeling bad about the change only because a lot of his side of the family didn't take it too well that I changed my name. I guess they took it as some type of disrespect or disowning them, but there was no need for any further explanation because I knew my reasons were justified. I also had slowly stopped coming around their house and neighborhood for numerous reasons. The main reason was because of the neighborhood being so bad and getting worse year by year, but also because I was kind of distancing myself and trying to establish my own true life. It was sort of severing ties, but still keeping contact with my close cousins over there who grew up with me and stayed in contact with me through it all.

I even remember my 2002 graduation at Norfolk State. My cousins, aunt, and my Nanny on Lopez's side showed up and surprised me. I was completely stunned, but because it was them and not him. I was excited to see that they had come all that way from Richmond to watch me cross the stage. It showed that they truly loved and supported me. This time I was damn sure going to graduate as someone other than Vincent Mapp; I was finally going to be Vincent Ellis White.

There were two in particular who I was very close to and decided to tell them of my finding my biological father. I was nervous and almost shaking all over, but I knew I had to get it off my chest. I've never been a person who wants to keep stuff bottled up inside, and this being the biggest secret in the world, I just knew I had to tell them. Would they believe me? Would they still embrace me as "cousin" or look at me like I'm no longer family?

These were some of the things that ran through my mind. I decided to tell them, but it was at the worst possible time. My nanny (named Ethel) had died. Yes, the same one who I spoke so highly of, the one who loved me un-conditionally, supported me in all the many things that I did in life, and that same sweet lady who assisted heavily in raising and protecting me while over on the treacherous West End side of things. Man, did I love her!

In the last few years (in all of my confusion) after finding out about Lopez, we hadn't been as close as we used to be when I was growing up over there, but I still loved her so much. I still called her grandma, my Nanny, so I knew I had to attend this funeral. I can't lie. There was a part of me that didn't want to go because I thought maybe Lopez would be there. Lo and behold, I was right!

I got to the funeral with my mother, and there he was front row with a correctional officer on each side of him. He had chains connected to his feet along with handcuffs. It was sad to see a grown man have to live that way. He was lucky they even let him out temporarily to see his own mother being buried, but even though he was out, he still wasn't free, not by a long shot.

There was a break in the funeral segment, and my two cousins and I went into another room just to chill. I decided this was my chance. I sat them both down and told them a big spill about how I have some real important news to tell them and I don't want them to disown me regardless of what I tell them. They kept reassuring me that they wouldn't, and I think they even saw my hands shaking. I went ahead and told them that I found out Lopez wasn't my biological father and that he beat on my mother for years, and that is why I changed my name. I pleaded with them that they wouldn't disown me! It was a big deal that I get to "keep them" so to speak. They were my two favorites. They embraced me, we all hugged, and said our 'I love yous." They said they will always see me as 'Lil'lo' their cousin.

After the funeral, everyone was standing outside. I was trying to hurry and sit inside the car so I wouldn't run into him. There was still a strong part of me that just couldn't let go of what he did to my mother and me; I hated to even think of him or see him. I used to tell myself that if he died, I wouldn't even go to the funeral. I didn't care who felt some type of way about it. I just didn't want to see him and have to give him a fake hug, so I sort of hid in the car. I'm glad that I did, because I saw him and my mother chatting right outside on the sidewalk briefly. She hugged him and he left, headed back with the two officers to his four walls-his cell. What a life for him!

A New Life

"A New Life"

Only our Lord could foresee|
A young child for you and me|
And among friends and family|
We celebrate a new life to be|
How my love has grown for thee|
And once I found out it was going to be a <u>he</u>|
An overwhelming joy just hit my eyes|
Just couldn't wait for the surprise|
Instantly began to envision my prize|
Tora, I knew he'd have your cheeks|
Maybe even your eyes| my eyebrows and smile|
And a nose no one can deny|
But just looking at you and I|
Our baby's beauty should be a given|
And right now I'm asking your permission|
Allow me to guide his way of living|
Be the <u>**man**</u> he looks up to|
One who he seeks for his strength|
And you will be our backbone|
Together, we shall blend|
To create such a wonderfully strong family|
Because in the mist of God|

We can do all things/

Perhaps JORDAN ELLIS WHITE can become the next
king.

Written by: Vincent Ellis White 2/18/2006 (Day of my son's Baby Shower)

March 5th, 2006, my first child was born-a boy. I am proud to

say that I was there during the entire pregnancy, as well as watched

(and even filmed) his actual birth. It was an experience that I will

never forget. Upon finding out that I would become a father, I remember wondering would my not having one consistent in my life ruin my potential as a great father? I later found out that it would actually serve as the fuel for me to become even greater than I would have ever imagined I'd be.

Maybe that is one of the main reasons that I tried real hard to be consistently active in the whole process. I used to do it all, from reading the "Expectant Father" books, to cleaning up the throw up from his mother's constant nausea, to making sure that I was at every doctor's appointment, to placing the earphones on her growing stomach and playing Mozart (we read/heard it helps children's senses develop better), and much more. I know that Lopez probably didn't do half of those things. I didn't have Chris Anderson there to do those things for my mother as I was being formed in her womb. I was highly proud of myself for being there and doing those things, among others.

I remember being so nervous at times and very excited as the months neared his tentative birth date. My fears of being a bad father had already passed. I made sure that I made it my personal business to be in my son's life always, no matter the cost or sacrifice that had to be made (and trust me, there were plenty that had to be made). I couldn't have him ever wondering where his dad was, who I was, or why I wasn't ever home or available to him. I wanted to be readily accessible to him at all times, and I made that my vow.

On the inside, I was deeply hurt that he wouldn't know who his grandfather was. I was hurt that I would probably have to bring him into my confusion. Do I ever even mention to him my whole "father" story? Am I shortchanging him? These were just a few questions that would come to linger in my mind during the pregnancy. I had prepared myself for the strong probability that he wouldn't ever know who his grandfather was-his "pa-pa."

After he was born, I did all of the daddy stuff. I changed diapers (struggled hard during the first few weeks), got up in the middle of the night to rock him back to sleep, sung to him, rocked him, fed him, played with him, took him to the mall with me, dressed him similar to how I dressed, prayed over him, and even the crazy stuff like helping pump the breast milk for him (which was the most confusing thing ever; I think we had a manual one at the time; mental note: never again). I knew that one day he would eventually start asking me questions about my father and where he was, so I made sure that he couldn't ever say that about me, plus it just felt natural to do all those things. I never thought in a thousand years that he'd have a grandfather to be there for him, like my grandfather "Billy" was there for me. Plus my mother had raised me right, in spite of my current circumstance.

Becoming a father just made my yearning for finding mine increase tremendously. I wanted advice. I still wanted answers. I still had questions. I felt so connected to my son that I wondered how someone could actually <u>not</u> feel the same way as I. I felt a new purpose in life. I now had a young one to live for and set a standard and example for. I had someone who would look to me for each decision of his young infant/toddler/adolescence stages of life. I now had a new life (due to him), even though many pieces of it were still shattered from me not having a father to call my own. It was bittersweet, but no one knew my struggles, my troubles, my pains, my worries, or my inner agony. I wanted to call someone Daddy, too.

Euphoria

She had finally found him-my real father. By God's grace, he had passed her in the hall of the same hospital that my grandmother was in for pneumonia. I thought about how glorious God is and how he made a way for me to get some of the confusion, anger, and fear cleared up. I remember I used to always wonder why I looked like I do, where I got certain traits and features from, and at the age of 27, she was telling me that she had found my father.

After crying all alone in the bathroom, I finally got myself together. I picked up the book and continued reading the last page. She went on to mention that he said he had another son, but he was locked up in upstate New York and that he was about 33 years old. "I have a brother?!?!?! WHAT?" I said out loud, but not to loudly. This was all just too much for me. Finding my Dad, a possible doctor, finding out I've had an older brother this whole time-aww man. I kept reading.

She wrote that he said he had four sisters, in which three of them still lived in the Mechanicsville area of Richmond. All of these newly found aunts, brothers, and such-I was amazed. I got on my knees and immediately thanked God for having His hand in it all, because it was and could only be through Him that this was all possible. She had his personal cell phone number written down at the bottom of that last page, so I definitely made sure I got his cell number out of it before getting up off of the ground. "Wow, I have my Dad's cell phone number" was all I could say to myself during my walk back down the stairs to my mom.

When I got to the bottom of the stairs, my mother was waiting for me. We made eye contact, and we hugged for what seemed like an eternity. She knew this touched me more than any gift ever could. We discussed it a bit, and she told me I should go call him and that he was awaiting my call; however, I was too nervous, so I waited until the day after. I called all of my closest friends and told them the whole story and the resulting good news. They were all crying by the end of the conversation because they knew how it all has always affected me throughout my life. They were very happy for me.

It was December 26, 2007, the next day, bright and early as I got up and just stared at my dad's (feels so good to say that and it be the right person) number sitting programmed in my cell. I got up enough nerve to call him.

"Hello" he answered on the first ring and shocked me.

"Uh, hey, Mr. Chris. This is Vincent, Belinda's son." I didn't really know what to say.

He said, "Yea, we have a lot to talk about, huh? You busy? Can you come over to the hospital, so we can sit down and talk?"

"Yea, I can, but I have my son, Jordan, with me. Is that cool?"

He said, "Sure you can, shoot, if what your mother is saying is correct, then that's my grandson."

We hung up. It was very awkward on the phone but he was willing to meet and that was a start. My hands finally stopped shaking temporarily.

Jordan and I arrived at Chippenham Hospital in about 10 minutes flat. I swear I must have done about 80+ on the freeway. It was amazing because I had been to that hospital over a thousand times and never had I seen him there. My mother did explain that he said he had lived in Florida for over 17 years, so maybe that's why she could never find him in the Social Services system and also why I never saw him there.

I texted him and told him we were downstairs in the lobby. He texted back and said he was on his way down. "Here comes the shaking again" I thought to myself. Jordan was only a one year old at the time, so he didn't know what was going on, nor did he know how monumental this event was going to be for him as well.

The elevator door opened. Out comes the very same brother that my mother described in the journal-my "gift.' Salt/pepper hair, strutting, smooth, slight build, short in stature, scrubs and uniform on, he walked right over to me as if he knew who I was. He stood there...we stared at each other...we shook hands... then we both sat down. I would have thought we'd at least have hugged, but I understood this was a complete shocker to him. I understood why he didn't embrace me like I would have wanted him to, but this was like a fairytale come true to me.

He sat down, leaned forward and just stared. I started smiling, because I could tell he was trying to read my face, checking out my features, my frame, etc. If he had any excitement, he sure didn't show it, but I did. I was excited and was doing the opposite of containing it.

Finally he spoke, and said "Hmmm, I can see it a little, but not all of the way." I understood his nervousness, but wanted to play it cool. I was trying to be cool in the midst of it all. It was crazy because he didn't know it, but he was playing it just like I would play it, moving just how I'd move. I was just watching him in amazement of how much we looked alike. I saw more than "a little." I saw my father. I finally saw where I got my chin, my complexion, my smile, and my eyebrows from. I saw myself all in his face, his cheeks, his facial structure, his frame, his swag, and more. I could just feel it. I knew ma wouldn't/couldn't have made a mistake on this one, not this time.

Ooooh, I had so many questions for him, but I kept it simple for the time being. I asked him how tall he was. he said "5'8."

I said, "Damn! Why couldn't I get that extra inch?" trying to lighten the mood and crack a joke (even though I meant what I said).

He laughed, and at that moment, I saw my own smile in him. I just stared in awe. I felt a tear trying to show itself, so I quickly pulled out the camera phone on my cell and told him I absolutely <u>had</u> to take a picture of him to show people, and guess what? He posed how I would pose. His cool smile looked effortless, as I've been told mine is. I looked at the picture that I had taken and then showed him. He smiled.

He then looked at me and said, "Damn, boy, you don't look like me as much, but you sure do look identical to my brother, Ricky, who died! My God!"

I just smiled, imagining what my Uncle Ricky was like before he passed. I wished that I could have known him.

He told me that he lives in Stafford, Virginia and commutes to Richmond every day (which is about an hour ride). He has four sisters (my aunts) in Mechanicsville, Virginia. He just kept saying that if this is true, he wishes he would have known (because he never knew about me). He just kept shaking his head while it was lowered, as if disappointed and saddened that this chain of events had to happen this way for us to meet. I thought I saw a tear forming in his eye as well. I told him that I know it is a lot to swallow, but I admired him for stepping up to be a real man. I told him of my many accomplishments, and I even gave him a free copy of my first book that I published locally entitled *Love, Life, and Religion: Reflections from the Soul* back in 2006. He was very impressed.

Then he said that he wanted a paternity test to rightfully determine things, but even if it doesn't come back positive, he still wanted to be in my life as a friend because he saw me going places.

I said, "I'm way ahead of you" and pulled out my research of several local paternity testing spots that we could go to and their prices. That gesture really touched me and showed me what type of man that I was dealing with which was a stand-up guy. He was calm, cool, laid back, but very smart, well-traveled, obviously making money, and most importantly, he was willing to be in my life regardless.

On my ride home, I had a million things running through my head. I couldn't wait to get that paternity test done to show him that we were father and son, and that we were destined to be together (even if meeting in such an awkward way). On December 28th, the next day, we met up to go take the paternity test.

99.99999999%!!

The paternity testing spot that we agreed upon was right on Midlothian Turnpike, which was a neutral location between both of our jobs. We met up at the testing area, got out of our cars, and we hugged. We walked up the stairs together, and I watched him as he walked. He walked like me (or was it that I walked like him?). My mind couldn't fathom how this was possible being that before yesterday, we had never met.

We got to the spot, and it was a small and very quaint office. We got inside, and we both looked around and then at each other. The simultaneous thought was that "this place looks hood." We were greeted by a middle-aged black woman in scrubs, and we introduced ourselves and told her about our appointment to be tested for paternity. She gave us some paperwork, and we sat down beside each other and began to fill it out.

My dad looked up and began to look around at the spot, and I could see his mind working. He started bombarding her with questions about the type of test we were about to do (I guess because he works in a hospital). I was shocked at how he was going in on her. Why do you use this? What's that for? When do we get results? Who are you certified by? What's your license? etc. He was definitely my daddy.

People say that I am so inquisitive all the time, and sometimes it urks them; however, the majority of the times it benefits me in the immediate or long run. I understood him for doing it. I started laughing, tripping out because I began to imagine me being like that at his age, in the early fifties.

I could tell she was getting fed up, but she stayed professional and answered all of his questions. She came over and swabbed both of our mouths with her testing tool. I was amazed at how modern things had gotten to be able to test for paternity without the mother even being there. My mother had told Chris that she was more than willing to take a test, but when I called this lady she said that now the testing can be done by a swab and with just two of those involved (i.e., daddy and son). She put the swabs in a plastic bag and sealed them both up together to be sent off to the testing lab, which was elsewhere. That was it. It was over. Nothing to it.

We left, both shocked at how quick and painless it was. We both went downstairs and sat outside for awhile just hanging like daddy and son would do. He began to tell me some stories from his childhood, growing up in the rough Jackson Ward area of Richmond (the same area that my grandmother on my mother's side grew up on). Richmond is very small, so it always amazed me to hear where people grew up at.

I listened and laughed my hardest as he told story after story, all ranging from how many girls he used to have, to dodging bullets, to hood fights, to obtaining his 2nd degree black belt (another coincidence because I am a 1st degree black belt), to his skin rash that he has on his body (the same that I carry on my neck and back), to his hernia he had as a teenager (I had one at the same age as he did), to many more. He was naturally hilarious! His storytelling ability was very reminiscent of my own.

People are constantly captivated by my stories, because I use my hands a lot to gesture. I project my voice up and down and tell jokes; I do it all. He did the exact same thing, and it blew my mind at yet another thing we had in common. We were bonding, whether he knew it or not, and I dug it hard.

We finally left and knowing that we had seven business days before we would get the results, we said we'd keep in touch. Every day that went by he'd text me something funny like; "Six more days to go, son. You ready to call me daddy officially now?" "Five more days to go, you sure you ain't heard anything yet?" "Four more days to go, you still got time to back out of this thing." He was hilarious to me. I guess how I was to others. Finally the 7th day fell upon us, and one by one we both received a call.

99.99999999%!!! The doc called and asked me, "Are you ready for your result of whether or not Mr. Chris Anderson is indeed your biological father?"

Nervously, I said, "Yes."

She said, "Well, he is 99.999999999999999% your father, and that's the highest percentage that one can be, so congratulations Vincent! I will also have an official letter here for you to pick up when you can. I have just called your father with the news, and he was highly excited. So, congrats again." OMG! I had already known that it was going to be that way, but to hear it is something else. Wow! I had officially found my biological father.

I called him, and he picked up yelling, 'Heeeyyy, son, I know you got the news. Maaan, you got to come over here to the hospital so everyone can meet MY SON!"

I loved how he dragged his words and had that signature Richmond slang and tone when he spoke, especially when he was ecstatic about a particular topic or scenario. It really felt good to hear him fully embrace me now. So, to the hospital I went.

I arrived in the parking lot and there he was, standing there waiting. I had told him the car that I'd be in, so he met me and said that he wanted to show me something special. I got out, and he walked me over to the other side of the parking lot and told me to close my eyes. When I got over there, he handed me something that felt like keys and told me to press the button in my hand and then open my eyes. When I opened my eyes, I couldn't believe what I saw. He was driving a freaking Rolls Royce antique car! I ran up to it and got inside. It looked like Paul Castellano's car, an Italian gangster mob boss's car. I loved it! I thought to myself, "This man is really caked up with dough."

He said, "Yeah boy, I figured since you are truly my son now, I can show you the prize car." He never ceased to amaze me. We walked inside, and when I arrived at his department in the cath lab of Chippenham, all of the surrounding doctors/RN, nurses and all were in full cheer mode. It felt like a full-fledged party.

My father was the life of the catheterization lab, and I learned that rather quickly. I was being passed around like a hot potato, each telling me tales of how awesome my father was, how much he runs things over there, how much he and I look alike (I loved to hear that), congratulating us on our discovery, and how much he was loved over there in his unit. It was amazing. Everyone was taking pictures of us, and we were posing like we do.

He said, with his arm around me, "Yeah, this is my son right here, and I can already tell that he is smooth like me."

I smiled, simply taking it all in. I had a new chapter in my 27-year-old life, which was just beginning. I thought to myself amongst all of the commotion, "God is such a miracle worker."

Super Bowl '08

Stafford, Va.

Dad invited me and some of my friends over to his house, which I called the "mini-mansion" because one look at it and you could tell he and his wife were getting money! It was two months later, and by this time we were tight as if we hadn't missed out on 27 years between each other. It was February, and everyone was talking about the big Super Bowl. He called me and asked me if I wanted to watch the Super Bowl at his house because he had a nice size TV that we all can watch and enjoy. I was like "Sure!" He told me to bring some of my friends, so I brought my god-sister, her boyfriend, and my best friend. They couldn't wait to meet him and to head out there, so we went north.

I followed the directions perfectly. When we pulled up to the house, all of our jaws dropped simultaneously. The house was gigantic. The yard even looked perfect. There were two big statues of lions on each side of the driveway. There was a stone water fountain in the middle of the yard for the birds. I saw the Rolls Royce again; my heart dropped again. I saw that he even had other cars. We got out and walked up to the door, all of us anxious.

Right when we got to the door, I rang the doorbell. I turned to my god-sister and said so that they all could hear, "Oh, by the way, don't be shocked, but he told me his wife is white" and turned back around smiling. That shocked everybody! Her jaw just hit the floor, but she had to rapidly pick it up because the door was about to open. Before they could even utter a word, the door opened and out came his wife, Gretchen. She was very pretty, and sure enough, she was white. I had wondered how she felt about it all since he told me that they had just married a year and a half ago, but he told me that she was very cool about it. He said that he called her on his ride home after he first found out about me, and she said, "Well Chris, check it out, and if he is indeed your son, then you got to be in his life." He said that he sent her a picture of me on his phone, and she wrote him back saying, "Yeah, that's your son." I remember thinking to myself, "Damn, that lady is too cool to be so accepting of such a thing." She welcomed us inside, and in that instant, we could see that we were indeed in paradise.

The outside did the house no justice at all. It was enormous. There were spiral stairs in the center of the living room. There was a big piano on the right and a wooden 50-piece wine holder on the left. The other part of the living room had the highest ceiling that I had ever seen. There were speakers all over the walls and plenty of flat screens posted everywhere. They had a sunroom and a kitchen that was immaculate. Even the kitchen had a built-in flat screen plus a flat oven inside the island. We were speechless; our facial expressions said it all.

As my dad showed us around, you could tell that he was very proud of his home. He described what he and Gretchen did versus what came with the house. He seemed to really love her. She had already prepared many hors d'oeuvres for us and had embraced me as family. It felt good. They took us out back. The yard was so spacious. He had a big pit bull, big cooking grills, a hammock, shed, and plans to add a pool very soon. It was awesome! He then took us upstairs and showed us more rooms that took our breath away. He had a Jacuzzi in his master suite with glass doors.

He took us all the way downstairs to his basement, and there was his own little Heaven. He had Redskins paraphernalia plastered all over the walls (but it was done tastefully). The stairs wound again as we went down. He had everything down there from dart boards on the wall, to a game room with pinball machines and casinos, three full bars, a huge pool table, three big slot machines, a popcorn machine and soda machine to match, a weight room with sauna, and finally, his theatre room.

We went inside the theatre room, and there was a big screen TV with a curtain cover like the movies. They had the movie seats with recliners and built-in cup holders, movie reels posted on the walls, and it looked just like United Artist theatres up in there. We couldn't believe our eyes!

Walking back out of the room, I began touching everything just like a kid would do. My god-sister and I played the slots. My best friend and I got started on a quick pool game, and my god-sister's boyfriend and I scanned the walls, looking and reading the many Redskins pictures he had up. He also had pictures of every popular professional player of a sport. He had more flat screens everywhere, just hanging up on the wall. It made no sense how hooked up his house was--the mini-mansion.

A few hours passed, and his house filled up quickly with many friends of theirs. We all got introduced, but he was extremely anxious to introduce me as his son. It felt good, but I felt a lot of his friends looking at me as if they were all thinking "where did you come from?" It was expected. When Super Bowl time arrived, we all gathered in the theatre room. We had a ball. Everyone was relaxed, reclined, and enjoying the food that Gretchen had prepared. She could cook! Later that night, we knew that we had to leave, but none of us even wanted to, because he had spoiled us so well. It truly felt like a big family that evening.

The Wedding That

Brought Us Together

April 2, 2008. My (newly found) cousin on his side was about to get married to her fiancé, and they were having the wedding at my dad's house. He invited me because he said that all of his family was going to be there. He had told them about me, so this was the best time to meet them all. I felt honored and nervous all at the same time. This was going to be my first time being able to meet everyone, and I remember being a little excited, nervous, having a little anxiety, trepidations, etc. As stated, he had already told everyone about me, so I wanted to live up to the hype. He had even asked me to write a poem for the wedding, since he knew that I could write poetry. I agreed.

When I arrived, the house was full of people that all shared similar features. My dad took me around and said, "Everyone, this is Vince, my son!" Everyone welcomed me. It reminded me of that movie Antwone Fisher after he found his family and they went to that big dinner. He had finally been able to meet the rest of his family on his dad's side, and so did I. Everyone accepted me. I finally got to meet my four aunts, one of which was an identical twin of my Dad's (I didn't know that).

I specifically remember my Aunt Sherrie, because she was the one that accepted me right off the bat. We hugged. We sat around the table and had some long and interesting talks. The crazy thing was that I found out that she used to work right beside my mother's old job that she retired from at AT&T for years (and by my other Aunt Valory). They never stopped to say hi or chat to be able to mention she had a brother named Chris Anderson. She reminded me of my Aunt Valory that passed so much. I think that's why we connected so well. I met all of my first cousins that day. Everyone was around the same age (lower thirties) and seemed to be very tight. They were all laughing with each other constantly, playing, fighting, and more. I met family from D.C. and saw cousins that I favored. I had pre-written a poem surrounding new love, and it was very good (even though I didn't even know the bride and groom). I had written the poem the next day after my father asked me to write it for the couple about to be wed.

We were having a ball, and the wedding was going to take place outside. Everything was setup so nice. It felt like I fit right in. I had on my beige-colored suit and was looking quite fresh. Everyone kept telling me how much I looked like my dad. I'd always just smile. The wedding had begun, and it was my time to recite the poem. I felt bad because I hadn't had the time to memorize it, so I had to read it from the paper. They printed it in the wedding bulletin though, so everyone was able to read along. As I read, I would occasionally look up for eye contact, and I remember reading people's lips. It was almost like reading their thoughts, as they would murmur to themselves, "Him and Chris look so much alike." I finished the poem and everyone loved it. It felt so good just to be a part of my cousin's wedding after just meeting them. Now, I was a part of their history.

At the reception (which was inside), everyone danced, drank, and laughed the night away. I played with my younger baby cousins and did a little two-step or too myself. I sat around and plenty of people that I didn't know were constantly coming up to me asking me how it felt to find him, how it feels now, and many questions about me. They asked about my mother, what I did for a living, and some even attempted to dig deeper into my personal life.

I told many about my hobbies, traits that were similar to my father's. I re-told the story. I brought them inside my world, even if just for a few minutes until they left for another drink refill. I shot pool with my dad, and for some games we tag-teamed as partners against some of his other guest. It was priceless. I stayed the night and departed in the morning, heading back to my hometown. I was Richmond bound.

December 20, 2008, the

Christmas Party

It was almost Christmastime again, and for this year I felt so high on life that I didn't need any gifts. I had mine, and he was named Chris Anderson. We had been text-crazed maniacs, laughing on the phone. I was visiting his job quite frequently, and he was even trying to groom me to join his field. He would invite me to watch countless surgeries being performed by him and his co-workers. He would suggest top-notch medical schools for me to apply to. No matter how many times I told him "That ain't my thing, Dad," he would keep trying. He wanted me to follow in his footsteps. I was actually considering it for a good minute, knowing that I had no interest in it whatsoever, just because he wanted me to. His co-workers were starting to get to know me. I would get hugs when I entered the hospital and more.

My dad was one for being the life of the party, so it was only natural that he would actually throw plenty of them-parties. He had an annual Christmas party, and I remember he had told me about the one from the previous year that I missed. He said that he wished we'd met before then so I could have come. He talked about how awesome it was. So when he invited me to the one for this year, I was ecstatic.

I went to the store Things To Be Remembered and got him a very classy (and expensive) plaque made that told me how happy and blessed I was to have him as my father. I blew up a nice picture of he and I that we took at the Doctors' Ball that he invited me to awhile ago the same year. I knew the picture would be very important because it was the first and only one that we had together. It was very special to me. We both had on our dressy outfits, mine a suit and his was a tuxedo. In the picture we really did look identical. Any stranger could tell that he was my father. We both had the biggest smile flowing in that picture. That was a beautiful night at the Science Museum. I knew he'd appreciate the picture being framed for him, so I had them both all wrapped up very nicely.

Dad told me his Christmas party was going to be on the Saturday before Christmas, and that everyone was going to be there again. I couldn't wait. Some of my cousins I had already exchanged numbers with, and we had been texting. I had been to some of my aunts' cookouts and brought my son along to play with their kids. I had been out to lunch and shared many conversations with my newly found closest aunt. It was party time.

When I got there, the house was loaded again. My dad sure could pack a house. I found him off somewhere telling his usual stories and jokes, cursing and painting a scene like no other. He was hilarious to me (and apparently to others still). My cousins (the newlyweds) showed up, and we all embraced. My aunts arrived. Dad's friends and neighbors all showed up, and everyone brought food. Gretchen had prepared amazing entrees, hors d'oeuvres, and later, dinner. They had a gigantic tree. We all sat around and opened gifts.

What almost brought me to tears was when I saw that everyone who was there had brought me and Jordan gifts. I told them they didn't have to do that because I knew we all had just met, but they did it anyway. Jordan was highly blessed at the Christmas party that evening, and he enjoyed every minute of it. I remember feeling so bad because I didn't get everyone a gift who got Jordan one, but they insisted that it was fine. My heart wanted to break a piece off so they could have it as a token of my gratitude. We truly felt loved.

Dad opened his gift, and he loved it! He looked like he wanted to drop a tear or two himself, but I know he wanted to maintain his "manly-man" stature. Everyone asked to see it, and they passed it around. Jordan and I had finally seemed like we fit right in, and it was truly a family affair. Once again, I felt like Antoine Fisher at the end of the movie when he was greeted by all of his new and recently-found family members (that's why that movie used to make me cry, I guess. No one truly knew my pain).

Dad's Birthday, 2010

It was March 3, 2010, and man, what a Wednesday it was. I had a rough day at work. I couldn't wait to leave early, so I could get off and go to the hospital to catch my Dad before he got off and drove all the way back to Stafford on his birthday. I remember even being shocked that he would work on his birthday. He seemed like the type that would take the whole week off for his birthday. I texted him and told him to stay put because I was going to be there around 4:30p.

This was very important to me, because he had been complaining to me about us slowly drifting apart the previous year due to our hectic work schedules. We barely talked or saw each other. I was working two jobs, had my son, was in school for my Master's degree, and writing books, He had two jobs. He worked at the hospital and had his own landscaping business back in Stafford. We were two little hustlers. So, this year I had made a promise to myself that I would try to step it up on my end, and hopefully he could follow. I got off early from work, already had my dad's gift in the trunk of my car, went to the hospital, and entered into the cath lab where he was working. I saw a bunch of balloons. Everyone seemed to have been celebrating all day for him, and he was all smiles as usual. When I came in, I was greeted with the same warm welcome I'd grown accustomed to. I gave him his gifts, he hugged me, we took pictures, and we celebrated. I chilled with him for over an hour. Then when it was time for him to leave, we walked and talked.

He shocked me when he began to reminisce about when he first found out about me that day from my mother. How when he saw me, he knew that I was his son but had to play it off until he saw the paternity test. He told me how he cried on the ride home because he couldn't believe that he had missed so much of my life, and it hurt him badly (he said he was mad at my mother for a bit but got over it). How he told his new wife and how happy he was, how proud of me he was in all my accomplishments and more...

He even told me something that completely blew my mind. He reminded me of a time when he and I were looking at some of my old pictures that I had, and I showed him a picture (the only one that I ever had) of Lopez. He told me that he had a confession to make. When I first showed him the picture of Lopez, he actually knew him. I remember gasping at the thought. He said they didn't know each other like that, but he knew him from shooting dice on the corners back in the day. He said that Lopez was popular in the West End, and he was in the Jackson Ward area where he was from. "I am constantly reminded of how small Richmond city is," I remember thinking to myself.

He was opening up to me, like a true father should always be able to do. I decided to open up as well. I told him about how tight my mother and I were, but the one thing that always caused a major conflict between us was when she would bring up the word "father." She could be talking about Lopez or finding Chris, but either way I'd sometimes just lash out. Then I told him how once I found out that he lived in Florida for so long and that most of the family on his side are in the medical profession (I found out that most of them are medical assistants, in school for nursing, LPN's, RN's, etc.), I felt disadvantaged or that I'd be shunned because I wasn't.

I always wondered if I had grown up with him in my life, would I have been in the same profession. I wondered would he think I was a failure because I didn't work in that same profession. As I told him this, he re-assured me that he was still very proud of me, though he would have liked to see me go into his same profession (as he smiled on the sly). I sincerely felt that he was indeed proud of me. That made the whole evening worthwhile.

He didn't drive the Rolls Royce this time, but he did give me a ride to my car in his new SUV. We sat in the car for a few minutes still taking a mind time-travel. Then I finally got out of the car. We hugged and told each other that we definitely needed this and to do it more often. Once I was in my car, he drove off. "Smooth like me," I said low so that only I could hear it.

The Past Shows

Its Ugly Head

My family from Raleigh, North Carolina, had come up to Virginia to visit. We all had decided to go to Lucille's to eat. Lucille's Southern Cuisine was a soul food spot over near Mechanicsville close to the Richmond airport. It was always jumping from what I heard over the years. I would never go for two reasons: 1) because it was too far, and 2) my mother had told me that Lopez had gotten out of jail earlier in the year and she found out he was working there.

"It ain't no way I'm ever going there then," I said aloud to myself when she told me that. When the family came, that was where they all wanted to go, and I was outnumbered. We got there, and I was nervous all over again. I had told my brother of the tales of Lopez, and he despised him the same. Acting tough as a young teenager would, he made me smile as he talked about what he would do if he sees Lopez trying to make a move towards my mother. We both smiled at the thought of having to react to something like that.

We got there, and I whispered to my brother, "Watch I bet you I will see him, because that's how my luck rolls." He said "You may not."

Low and behold my luck, as soon as we walked completely inside, my eyes locked on my Mr. Lopez, the free man. He was just where my mother said he'd be--working in the kitchen. When he saw all of us coming in, he immediately came out and greeted us. I watched as he hugged my mother (again), shook my uncle's hand (her brother, who couldn't stand Lopez growing up; they had a constant beef), greeted my aunt, and even shook little Jordan's hand.

"Come here, J," I said, and Jordan came back over to his Daddy.

Lopez looked up at me from him bending down, and said (in his usual Richmond city West End slang) "Heey maan, long time no see; gimme a hug." Before I could say the original thought that what was in my head (which was "hell nah"), he had pulled me in. I noticed how strong he had gotten from being in jail. His physique was still a small frame, but he had what they called, that "man strength." I didn't let him hug me for long. He had small talk with my mother and brother. Then he went back to his cooking.

My mother had always told me how he was a good cook, and that he could sing very well (though I don't remember getting one home-cooked meal from him, receiving any singing lessons, nor hearing an angelic voice flow from his mouth). We sat down at our tables, and from where we were sitting, I could still see him.

It obviously still bothered me to even see the man, and it had been over 12 years since I found out about his true lifestyle and the abuse he put my family through. My mother had moved on and received her closure a long time ago she said, when she "gave it to God." Then she said that's when later he blessed her with finding Chris. That was the best gift that God could have ever given to me in this life besides His son and my son. I knew that I had to simply be grateful and learn to get over the pain and hatred that I still harbored for this man. By the grace of God, my life was going very well. I was very blessed and highly favored, had many accomplishments, and grew up surrounded by love. I had even found my real father who was an amazing man. We were growing closer every year that passed by.

Some months had passed, and we hadn't been to Lucille's in awhile. We went to a new local soul food spot named Mama J's, which was in Richmond's downtown area. My mother ran into an old friend of hers who she knew from her "Lopez era." He surprised her with some newly found info regarding Lopez. He said that he heard Lopez was locked up again, and that it was going to be awhile before he gets out. Why did that news still interested me? I wondered. I didn't know, but it secretly still did interest me a little.

When my mother told me what the guy told her, I started asking mad questions. "What!?! What did he do? How long did he get? etc. My mother didn't really care what he did or how much time he received. She said if he went back in, then she knew he probably had a lot of time due to him being a habitual offender. We discussed how sad it was that he just kept going back and forth, in and out of the prison system. I said that he'd probably die in there, but ma didn't respond. I counted my blessings that I didn't follow his path, and that I kept my word about never going back behind a cell again.

The following week, I decided to be extra curious and look him up on the computer. I found out that he had quite a few charges, some stuck and some were still pending. They were certified with a grand jury, so I couldn't see all of them, but I saw enough of them to make up my mind that he was done with his life as a free man--this life. He had charges in the City, as well as the County of Chesterfield. He has some of the same exact charges that he had done time for way back in the 80's. I guess some people never change or rehabilitate.

I didn't believe that I still hated him at all, but I must admit that I felt mixed emotions inside because there was a part of me that smiled and a part of me that felt bad for the guy when I read all the charges he faced in my city. He was appealing them, but I knew he wasn't going to win. He probably knew it, too. He was about to go right back to the place that he knew all too well--his home. The rhetorical question popped itself in my head, "Sometimes the past does know how to rear its ugly little head, doesn't it?"

Irony

Fast forward, it was August 24, 2010, and I had just received the emergency call that my one and only grandmother had driven herself to the hospital due to having some chest pains. Of course, I rushed to the hospital with all kinds of thoughts bursting through my medulla, in which also saturated the rest of my brain. Little did I realize that this was very similar to my 2007 experience when she got sick and became bed ridden in Chippenham Hospital, and I ended up finding Chris, my father.

As I arrived and ran to check on her, she was sitting up and looking very relaxed. Needless to say, it eased my nerves a bit. My family was there, everyone from my ma, to my cousin Binky, my Uncle Ellis, and my best friend, Cory (who might as well be family). Off and on folks left and came in, all awaiting the test results.

We found out how much of a miracle worker God really is. She had driven herself there for chest pains, but when the test came back, there were no signs of anything relating to her chest. However…they had now found a severe aneurism in her stomach. It crushed me! They were consoling me saying she'd be okay and they'd just need to have surgery to remove it, but this was my grandmother. I just couldn't handle it at the time.

The doctors mentioned something about life support for the surgery, and I couldn't hold it any longer. I broke down, right in front of everyone. I had to be taken out of the room by my mother, and on the way out, I smashed the wall with my fist. I told God that it wasn't fair. My mother told me of God's goodness and that He would pull her through this one just like in 2007, but I didn't really hear her. My heart hurt.

She sent my best friend, Cory, over there to me next with hopes that he'd have better results, and she was right. He consoled me, but afterwards he brought in the laughter. We laughed about so much that I forgot about the major concerns of the surgery. Laughter is truly the cure to any pain.

Now, my father, Chris, also worked at Chippenham in the catheterization lab, so I called him. I told him that this was my only grandmother and that I needed him to be checking in on her at the times when we weren't or couldn't be there. I needed him to double-check behind the doctors just to make sure everything was going

173

smooth, and that the proper things are being done to ensure a successful outcome.

Dad said, "I got you, son. I'm going to make sure she's straight." Every day that passed, one of us were there to sit with my grandmother and keep her spirits up (as well as our own). I was trying to be strong for her sake, but there were a few times that she caught me breaking down. Just the thought of what she was facing frightened me over and over. Her age of 80, her serious emphysema/low oxygen, and having to face such a detrimental surgery for this aneurism, it was all just too much.

I remember how she touched my heart when she said with a smile, "Your dad has been coming in here quite often to check on me." Oh, the irony. He was doing it out of the sheer kindness and thoughtfulness of his heart. The last time she was laid up in the hospital, my mother had walked right up on this man who helped create me and told him that he had a 27-year-old son. Three years later, Chris Anderson was checking up on my grandmother and calling to console me, his blood, his spitting image of a son. Now this time, he was assisting my grandmother daily and making sure she was good at the times when we weren't there.

Her surgery was done on that following Tuesday, August the 31st. It was successful, and my dad had called me three times that day just to check on me. I told him that the doctors said she did very well, and that they were proud of her. So were we.

He said, "I knew she would pull through. She's a trooper." I just smiled. She recovered pretty quickly, and the doctors let her go home in just three days after the surgery. The entire family rejoiced in the Lord and how good He had been to us.

My mother came to pick me up to take me out to lunch, so we hit the Croaker's Spot which was another popular soul food joint. We sat and shared jokes, laughter, and good fun. We tripped on how my grandmother was so emphatic about getting home to make my best friend, Cory's, wedding that was rapidly approaching (it was all she talked about). We chuckled about how my grandmother played her favorite song over and over and over again for the duration of her stay: *"Marvelous"* by Walt Hawkins (I will never forget that song!)

We laughed at how my father was always so cool as he strutted in her hospital room to check on her and how he always made her laugh. It was her first time ever meeting him since I found him. Oh, the irony. I thought it was enough irony for me to handle when I first obtained a job at the very same Social Services building that my mother had gone to find him, but this simply took the cake. I truly believe it was God's divine plan to bring us all together.

Just then, before we finished up our meals, my Blackberry buzzed my hip. It was my father sending me a text saying "If you're not busy this weekend, you should come to the house. We're having a cookout, and you know I'm going to need my son there to make it complete."

"Well, alright then," I thought to myself. "Gotta love that." "You got it, pop, love you." I hurried and sent back to him via text. I smiled at my mom, and she knew what that smile meant--that it was my daddy.

Her dream had come true as well, all because she had given the situation to God. All of the guilt that my mother carried around within, the pain, and so much more. I know it felt good that she was finally freed. I was finally free, of confusion, and my grandmother was even freed of her temporary misery. My father has his youngest son in his life now. Finally...true tranquility.

Equanimity after Life's Ongoing Storm

Poetry Inspired By These Events...

"Teardrops of Hope"

Should've known he'd never leave me/
God guided me right to you/
Though it felt 27 years to late/
He's always on time as usual/
His own clock, in which we just don't have access to/
He's lifted some of the pain, that in excess grew/
And grew, and grew, family and friends hardly,
knew/
It was hidden so well, but I knew my justice was due/
Now I stare at the creator of my flesh and bones
down/
Teardrops of hope, finally begin to flow now/
From a space in my eye that they could call home/
I can crack a smile now, remove the frown built from
stone/
Slowly push out the question mark that stayed
afloat/

Inside my mind, cruising like an empty boat/
Without a compass, or lines of longitude and latitude
to coast/
The built up anger/ "How could I miss a stranger?/ I
would boast/
A ticking time bomb being pushed to blow/
However, God knew my destiny was ordained/
I had to endure the emotional pain/
The thought of never seeing my biological father
again/
Or even a first time, because all I had was a name/
Now, I can pick up the phone, or visit that very same
man/
The Almighty Lord and Savior, devised a well
thought out plan/
My teardrops of hope can finally land.

Written By: Mr. Vincent White ©2008

"Daddy"

I want my son to be proud of his Daddy/
I want my Daddy to be proud of his son/
Because before December '07/
My daddy thought he only had one/
Once he found out he really had two/
His heart spread out & instantly grew/
He found a whole new space/
And his soul created more room/
A piece of him now dwells within me/
It always did, but now I'm able to physically see/
He's now able to give enormous portions of his love/
To the youngest son that he helped to conceive/
Though we just met/
He's proud of the accomplishments that I've
achieved/
& I'm proud that we were able to finally meet/
More confirmation that our God is truly Almighty/
He allowed me to reach the light down the road of that
tunnel/
It started wide, then went narrow like a funnel/
My own son entered the world & I was given a new
path/

To walk more righteously & become the greatest Dad!
To be a great role model for him & make his life
better!
He changed my outlook on life on so many different
levels!
I now put him first before all of my endeavors!
I now strive for more when planning my goals!
Within two glorious years!
These two new males have both entered my soul!
I pray that their relationship can grow close!
Just as Jesus has made such a beautifully paved
pathway for each of us.

Written By: Mr. Vincent White ©2008

Beloveds,

I pray that this memoir will inspire others' faith to be replenished, inspire broken families to be restored and brought back together, reduce bickering, lies and deception, and produce honesty between families and amongst each other. This book is for anyone who's ever thought a parent was one thing or type of person and found out they were another, been caught in a nasty whirlwind of family lies, been disappointed by someone in or close to their family, or didn't even know who their real/biological parents were.

I want each of you all to know that God is still in the miracle-working business. He can make a way where you thought there would never be any. I purposely did not celebrate any Father's Days until I found Chris, my biological father (besides my first Father's Day as a father in 2006). I didn't see a need, because in my eyes I didn't have a father. I never thought in a million years that I'd ever find or even meet my biological father, and now we talk, share laughs, and spend time together on a daily basis.

Now, I no longer yearn for that fatherly figure. I no longer live with unanswered questions about my family and heritage. God made this all possible for me. He provided me with true tranquility. Don't ever give up hope. There is power in prayer and having faith.

-Vincent Ellis White, MED.

Acknowledgements:

I would like to thank God from whom all blessings have been bestowed unto me. This has truly been the biggest and most visible miracle that I have had the opportunity to be a part of firsthand and witness. This is my testimony. If there is anyone who may not believe that my God is real, your mind should be changed by the end of this book. I just want to thank you, Lord, for such a blessing. Lord, thank you for clearing up the unlimited amount of questions that have spiraled through my head for 27 years.

I want to thank my mother, Belinda, for being a praying mother. You are truly a prayer warrior and soldier for Christ. You are the reason that I have made it this far in my life. You reared me with spiritual and motherly guidance, you kept me in church ever since I was born, you led by example, and you loved me more than anyone in the whole world. Even though I was missing a father, you always made it so I would never have to go without, and you did it all without any help (besides my grandmother and aunt). Thank you for never giving up, for knowing how to give a situation to God and let it be, loving me unconditionally, and lastly, for allowing me to express myself through this memoir. It truly is my therapy. I love you beyond measure. You will always be my rock.

Thanks to my brother, Devon, just for being there for me and not judging me when I made those typical "big brother" mistakes. Love you, bro! Keep your head towards God.

To my son, Jordan Ellis White, please know that I do it all for you. You are the light of my life, and daily you give me reason to do what I do and move how I move, which is filled with passion and drive to succeed. I want to lead and pave the way for you. I, as your father, am here to set the example for you, and any/all of my actions have such a powerful impact on your way of thinking and life in general. So, again I thank you for being the world's greatest son and keeping Daddy on his toes. I simply love how your face lights up whenever I come to pick you up, or come to one of your events (or you to one of mine), or when we are playing. I love how we have no problem saying "I love you" several times a day and hugging it out like family is supposed to. I absolutely love how you are truly a one of a kind little man who already loves the Lord at such an early age. I also love how you are always smiling and full of spunk, and I know that I have myself and your mother, Latora, to thank for that. With both of our outgoing personalities, I think we knew that you'd be a laughing riot. God has truly blessed us both, and I just want to continue doing my part as your father by consistently showing you the Christ in me. I love you.

Next, I absolutely must thank my grandmother, Quincilee, White. Grandma, you've held down every position imaginable in my life and passed on so much of your wisdom along the way. I just want to tell you that you are my heart, and you know how I feel about you. I don't know what I'd do if anything ever happened to you. You know how close we are, so I need you to just keep on keeping on for your #1 grandson, Lil'Lo (you have to see my son,

Jordan, graduate)!. You're 82 years old, but I swear I can't tell the way that you maneuver through the streets of Richmond daily, so live on!

I want to thank my family in Raleigh, North Carolina-Brandon, Shannon, Justin, Aunt Gwen and Uncle Ellis (Boo-Boo). I want to give a special shoutout to my cousin, Binky, thanks, Mr. Ellis White III, for all of your support, input, promotion, and genuine love for your "cuzzo!" I love each of you all (you know us Ellis's have to stick together)! I also want to thank my best friend (and favorite Richmond city firefighter), Cory Wilson, and God-sister, Jennifer Nicholson (and the whole Nicholson family, which is like my own), just for supporting me endlessly and being there during the findings of my biological father and watching (as well as playing a part in) my growth and evolution. I have known you both for a lifetime (like brother and sister), and you two continue to inspire, encourage, and push me to strive for greatness. Let me also take this time to thank my photographer, Jerry Fain of Broxtan Photography (Broxtanphotography.netau.net), for doing such a wonderful job on the cover and the author photo for this book. I'd also like to thank my editor, Jacqueline Duresky, of Best Secretarial Services for editing this memoir.

I'd like to thank the man that I've been in dire need to find to be able to fulfill certain parts of my life-Mr. Chris Anderson, my father. Thank you for being receptive to my mother on that special day (and not running away) and for being willing to get to know me (your son) and even my son, Jordan, (your grandson). We love you. Just as my son and I are inseparable, I pray that you and I can get that way as well. You are truly a stand up man's man in my book. I pray that God continues to work on your heart, mind, and soul. I also pray that we can continue to grow closer and closer in this precious life together. I want to experience trips, pictures, memories upon memories, inside jokes, and all that a father and son can share, until we both leave this earth. We still have plenty of time. I love you with all of my heart.

Lastly, I want to thank the entire Anderson family for embracing me. To all of my loved ones (too many to name), I love each of you. Big shout out to my older brother, Chris White. Hold your head; see you soon.

It's all about family togetherness. God is love.

To Calandra Davis, I just want to say that I have so much love for you and thank God for you being in my life. I know you arrived on the scene after this book was created, however you have still chosen to support me with every idea and vision that I've thrown at you. You are a true example of what a real virtuous woman of God should be.

I also want to give a big shout to Omar Moore and Dominic Davis, my next two closest friends from Norfolk State. Man, you two guys have been through the fire with me and made it back alive! I've known both of you since 1998, and we've always stayed close. Now we all are doing big things in life (and staying positive in the process). Omar, you are about to become a lawyer next year (congratulations, my brother), and Dominic, you already have your own successful production company, Dreamclip Productions. I am sincerely proud, and I love you all.

Also, to my close comrade, James Winston, I give thanks. Thank you for constantly praying for me and keeping me encouraged and uplifted every time that we spoke. We have been friends since WAY back, and let me just say, look at what God hath done! Also to I'esha Hornes (the Gap Tooth Diva, thank you for setting the example of what it's like to push yourself and keep the motivation), Duron Chavis (Brother Manifest, keep teaching & preaching brother, you are a genius), Jenee' Murphy (you have been one of my biggest supporters from the beginning, and I thank and love you from the bottom of my heart; I owe a lot to you. Let's let the past be the past because the future is bright for the both of us. You have been a true angel in my life. Nuff' respect due.), Latasha Thoms (you put me on son! My fellow author), Mark-Anthony Tynes, Mary Coward, Neecy, Shana, Sharvette Mitchell (my Co-Host!), Shirley (Muir and Watkins), Tam Whitaker, Tee Arties, Lamar T., Taunya Jones (very good friend, thanks again for all of your support over the years. Love you), Ellen Ann Smith Sudderth (Second momma!) and Nikkea Smithers (thanks to you both for bringing me under your literary wing), Jamila Joy and Maressa D. (you two are the ones that got my name buzzing in the city of Richmond; I love you two guys) and so many more that I absolutely can't name. I thank each of you all for playing a significant part in my life up until this point. You all help me to grow, and your contributions help to nourish me like a plant so that I can continue to bloom and blossom. God has truly blessed me with some amazing friends and family members.

I'd like to personally thank all of my fans, my IShoutforJoy staff, also those that I've ministered to, testified in front of, and those close to me that have actively pushed me to finally write this very personal book. It is with much humbleness that I say I owe it all to you all.

Let me be clear….and thank Mr. Lopez "Big Lo" and let you know that I FORGIVE YOU. Though I don't agree at all with the choices or actions that you made, I thank you because in some way, shape, or form, you became inspiration for me. God's <u>ultimate</u> divine plan is unimaginable, unexplainable, and amazing at the same time! I've also learned that for this book to fully be blessed, I MUST forgive you.

Let me also take the time to thank my church family at Future Church of Christ Holiness in Richmond, Virginia, for always supporting my endeavors, helping me to utilize my gifts, showing me unconditional love, and for just trying to get me into Heaven. Thanks, Bishop Nicholson, you've always been there when I called (and I called a lot in the beginnings), and you helped mold me into a fine young man. You taught me the importance of living holy. I thank each of you all....

Contact Info:
Web: http://www.lifelovereligion.com
http://www.facebook.com/TheVincentEllisWhiteShow
Twitter: LifeLoveRVA
Email: llrpublishing@yahoo.com
Cell: (804)852-0449

Dad's Picture:

Chris Anderson

Dad's Birthday

This was a very special day because this was the day that I brought my newly written book *The Fully-Seasoned Man's Relationship Recipe: [Men's Confessional/Women's Tutorial]* to my pops. When my dad saw the book, he immediately bought one and went home and read it. He came back to me in about a week's time, and was just bragging about how good it is and how proud he is of me. He was so impressed by my writing skills that he ended up going all around the hospital where he works at and generating sales and making transactions for me. With my father's help, I received an additional 25 sales. He's the best!

Mother & Son

This is the very first picture that my daddy and I took

together after meeting! It is my favorite picture of us because it was

the first, it showcases how much we look alike (everyone has said

that we look like twins in this picture), and we both look very

debonair. I was so happy to be with him on this night. He had a

ball/dance to attend that his job always has once a year at the science

museum in Richmond and he invited me and my then girlfriend at

the time to come along and accompany him and his wife Gretchen. I made sure I looked good that night because this was my *coming out* night as I knew everyone would be asking him who I was and where did I come from ha-ha. We took this picture and it came out so well we had it blown up in both of our houses.

***Romans 8:28** "And we know that all things work together for good to them that love God, to them who are called according to his purpose." *

CPSIA information can be obtained
at www.ICGtesting.com
Printed in the USA
FFOW04n1409190617
36802FF